The Journey

Walking the Road to Bethlehem

Expanded Paperback Edition

The Journey
Walking the Road to Bethlehem

The Journey
978-1-5018-2879-9
978-1-4267-4646-8 *eBook*
978-1-61045-459-9 *CD Audiobook*
978-1-5018-3604-6 *Large Print*

The Journey: Leader Guide
978-1-4267-5332-9

The Journey: DVD
978-1-4267-1999-8

The Journey: A Season of Reflections
978-1-4267-1426-9
978-1-4267-4649-9 *eBook*

The Journey for Youth
978-1-4267-2858-7
978-1-4267-5891-1 *eBook*

The Journey Children's Study
978-1-4267-2857-0

For more information, visit JourneyThisChristmas.com.

Also by Adam Hamilton

24 Hours That Changed the World

Christianity and World Religions

Christianity's Family Tree

Confronting the Controversies

Creed

Enough

Final Words from the Cross

Forgiveness

Half Truths

John

Leading Beyond the Walls

Love to Stay

Making Sense of the Bible

Not a Silent Night

Revival

Seeing Gray in a
    World of Black and White

Selling Swimsuits in the Arctic

Speaking Well

The Call

The Way

Unleashing the Word

When Christians Get It Wrong

Why?

For more information, visit www.AdamHamilton.org.

ADAM HAMILTON

The Journey
Walking the Road to Bethlehem
Expanded Paperback Edition

Abingdon Press
Nashville

The Journey
Walking the Road to Bethlehem
Expanded Paperback Edition

This book is printed on elemental chlorine-free paper.
ISBN 978-1-5018-2879-9

Photos courtesy of Alex Schwindt and Adam Hamilton.

16 17 18 19 20 21 22 23 24 25 — 10 9 8 7 6 5 4 3 2 1
MANUFACTURED IN THE UNITED STATES OF AMERICA

To the thousands of people at The United Methodist Church of the Resurrection who embody the Christmas story by giving sacrificially to serve and bless others in Christ's name. I am humbled and proud to serve as their senior pastor.

Contents

Introduction

Welcome to *THE JOURNEY.*

In some ways this book is a prequel to another book I wrote, *24 Hours That Changed the World.* In that book I explored the final day in the life of Jesus Christ, starting with the Last Supper and ending with Jesus' death and burial, including a postscript focused on his resurrection.

In *The Journey,* I've taken the same approach to the Gospel stories surrounding the birth of Jesus. I've drawn on the insights of scholars, historians, theologians, and archaeologists to help you read the Bible accounts with fresh understanding. I traveled to the Holy Land to rediscover the stories in the places they occurred, starting in Nazareth where Mary learned she would give birth to the Christ. I then went to Bethlehem, Joseph's hometown, where he probably was living when he learned that Mary was pregnant. Next I visited Ein Karem, the traditional site of Elizabeth and Zechariah's home, where Mary spent the first three months of her pregnancy. I walked portions of the road

Mary and Joseph may have taken as they were forced to travel to Bethlehem in the ninth month of Mary's pregnancy. Finally I completed the journey by returning to Bethlehem, where Jesus was born.

I wrote this book anticipating that people might read it in the weeks leading up to Christmas, the season Christians call Advent. With that in mind, I've written four weeks of reflections to accompany this book, in a little volume called *The Journey: A Season of Reflections*. The reflections invite readers to see their daily lives through the lens of Jesus' birth. While in the Holy Land retracing the steps of Mary and Joseph, we also created a series of videos so that readers could see Nazareth, Ein Karem, and Bethlehem for themselves. A small-group leader's guide accompanies the videos for those reading the book with friends.

My hope and prayer is that in reliving the story of Jesus' birth, you will experience the "good news of great joy for all the people" that comes from knowing the true meaning of Christmas.

–Adam Hamilton

The Journey

Walking the Road to Bethlehem

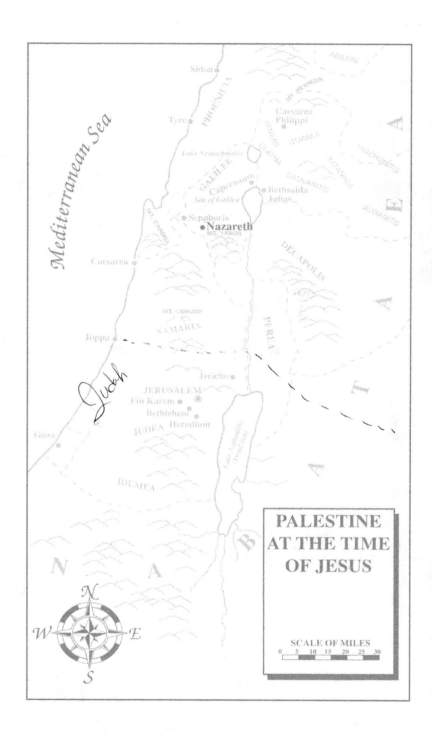

PALESTINE
AT THE TIME
OF JESUS

SCALE OF MILES
0   5   10   15   20   25   30

1. Mary of Nazareth

In the sixth month the angel Gabriel was sent by God to a town in Galilee called Nazareth, to a virgin engaged to a man whose name was Joseph, of the house of David. The virgin's name was Mary. And he came to her and said, "Greetings, favored one! The Lord is with you." But she was much perplexed by his words and pondered what sort of greeting this might be. The angel said to her, "Do not be afraid, Mary, for you have found favor with God. And now, you will conceive in your womb and bear a son, and you will name him Jesus. He will be great, and will be called the Son of the Most High, and the Lord God will give to him the throne of his ancestor David. He will reign over the house of Jacob forever, and of his kingdom there will be no end." Mary said to the angel, "How can this be, since I am a virgin?" The angel said to her, "The Holy Spirit will come upon you, and the power of the Most High will overshadow you; therefore the child to be born will be holy; he will be called Son of God. And now, your relative Elizabeth in her old age has also conceived a son; and this is the sixth month for her who was said to be barren. For nothing will be impossible with God." Then Mary said, "Here am I, the servant of the Lord; let it be with me according to your word." Then the angel departed from her.

(Luke 1:26-38)

IT IS ONE OF WESTERN CIVILIZATION'S best-known stories. For two thousand years it has been told and retold, preached and sung about. It has been represented by the titans of art and by the purveyors of mass-produced lawn figures. We celebrate it every year with Christmas trees and lights, with gifts and cards, carols and hymns.

Even if you did not go to church growing up, you're probably familiar with the story. You know the locale—a manger in Bethlehem. You know the cast of characters—Mary and Joseph, the angels and shepherds, the wise men and King Herod. You may know plot details—the census, the long journey, the overcrowded inn.

And yet, as is often the case, the story's very familiarity may keep us from fully grasping its riches. We think, "Well, yes, I know that story," as its depth and nuance escape us.

There is much more to the Christmas story than meets the eye. There are details we may have missed entirely. And there are certainly a few places where the picture you have in your mind's eye is actually wrong!

The purpose of this book is to explore the story of Jesus' birth with fresh eyes and ears. We will walk through the Holy Land and retrace the steps of those involved. We will draw upon insights gained from historians, archaeologists, biblical scholars, and theologians and from walking in the places the story occurred, all in an effort to discover the real meaning of Christmas.

In seeking that meaning, we will address four questions:

—What actually happened leading up to and including the first Christmas?
—What does the story teach us about the character of God?
—What does it tell us about the child whose birth we celebrate?
—What does this story mean for our lives today?

We will address those questions in each chapter, as we deal with every piece of the story, in an attempt to come to a deeper understanding of what the Christmas story teaches us about Jesus Christ and about God's will for our lives.

Nazareth

The Christmas story begins in the town of Nazareth nine months before the birth of Jesus. Now, if any narrative ever cried out for attention to detail it is this one, so it's worth taking a good look at this little town and what it might tell us about the nature and character of God.

Nazareth is much more widely known today than it ever was in Jesus' day. It is not among the sixty-three villages of Galilee mentioned in the Hebrew Talmud or the forty-five mentioned by first-century Jewish historian Josephus, who knew the area well. This was an insignificant little town. Its population is estimated to have been between one hundred and four hundred people, though its lack of mention in the Talmud and by Josephus might suggest that it was far smaller.

In telling a stranger about Nazareth, a native might well have mentioned the large nearby town of Sepphoris, which had a population of thirty thousand and was well known. Sepphoris was comparatively affluent, with culture, shopping, and undoubtedly all the other things expected of a prosperous town. Excavations have shown us luxury villas with extravagant tile mosaic floors. Nazareth, on the other hand, had few of these things. It was likely a town of farmers, shepherds, and laborers who walked an hour each way to sell their goods and services in Sepphoris. These were not affluent people by any means. In fact, evidence shows that, far from living in luxury villas, some of them may actually have built their homes within and around the area's soft limestone caves—the least expensive form of housing in the first century and a sign of relative poverty.

Nazareth's low social status is seen in John 1:45-46 when Philip, one of Jesus' first disciples, told his friend Nathanael, "We have found him about whom Moses in the law and also the prophets wrote, Jesus son of Joseph from Nazareth." Nathanael said to him, "Can anything good come out of Nazareth?"

As I picture a place like Nazareth today, I imagine one of the hundreds of little towns in Kansas—towns without a stoplight, with no high-speed Internet, no restaurant or nightlife, not even a grocery store. The children travel to the next town over for school. No one puts on airs in these towns. They're just good, honest, hard-working people. This is what I imagine when I picture Mary's hometown.

Living Water

Nazareth was likely founded at least a couple of hundred years before the time of Jesus by people who had come to the area looking for work and the chance to make a new start. Such people generally started towns where there was water, and there was a spring on the site that became Nazareth. Mary would have grown up fetching water from that spring, and in fact it still flows today. (In biblical times spring water—cool, clean, and bubbling up from the earth—was referred to as "living water.")

As the town was built up over the centuries, it rose above the spring so that, in order to see it today, visitors must descend below ground level inside the Greek Orthodox Church of the Annunciation near downtown Nazareth. (In the video designed to accompany this book, I show you this site and most of the other places I'll be mentioning.)

I can't help but think that Jesus, who spent thirty years of his life in Nazareth, drew on the memory of that spring when he spoke to his disciples of living water and when he said to the woman at the well, "If you knew who you were talking to, you would ask of me and I would give you living water and you would never thirst again." (See John 4:10.) Jesus knew, as did the people who founded his hometown at the site of that spring, that water is life, and he knew the blessing of living (spring) water.

As the name of the church on that site indicates, Orthodox Christians believe it was there, while drawing water, that Mary received word from the angel Gabriel that she would bear the Christ Child. (*Annunciation* means "announcement.") As a result, many Christians believe that the mystery of the Incarnation—God taking on human flesh—begins there.

As I listened to and watched the spring water coming up from the ground below the Orthodox Church of the Annunciation, I was reminded of Jeremiah 2:13, where God said that "my people have committed two evils: / they have forsaken me, / the fountain of living water, / and dug out cisterns for themselves, / cracked cisterns that can hold no water." Is it merely a coincidence that God, who called himself the "fountain of living water," might have chosen the spring of Nazareth as the place where Mary would become pregnant with a child who would one day refer to himself as the giver of living water (John 4:10)?

Did Mary Live in a Cave?

Roman Catholics mark the site of the Annunciation not at the spring, but at what tradition says are the remains of Mary's house, located several blocks away. From the late 300s, churches have been built on this location. The current building, the Basilica of the Annunciation, completed in 1969, is a modern structure built of concrete and has two levels. The upper level houses the nave of the church—its main sanctuary. Near the altar is a large opening that looks down to the lower level—the church's holiest place. When visitors descend the stairs to the lower level, they come to a cave or grotto that is said to be the home of Mary and, according to Roman Catholic tradition, is the location where Mary offered herself to God; and "the Word became flesh."

It strikes some visitors as odd that Mary's family would have lived in a cave, or that at least part of her home would have been in a cave. But caves occur naturally throughout the Holy Land. The soft limestone is easily hewn to expand the cave, adding additional rooms and even shafts for light. You can still find people in Nazareth using caves for their homes, for storage, or even as shelter for their animals.

In case you're still not convinced that people lived in caves, a quick study of the Old Testament reveals that Lot lived with his daughters in a cave (Genesis 19:30) and King David is said to have lived in the "cave of Adullam" (1 Samuel 22:1 and 2 Samuel 23:13).

As we will see, many of the important traditional holy sites in Israel and the Palestinian territories are grottoes or caves. It is possible that the cave was merely the "basement" of a home that was built above ground but later destroyed. (The cave said to be Mary's home has stairs leading up from the cave to an upper level.) But in some cases the cave may have been the entire home.

My ninety-five-year-old great aunt recently showed me a photo of a farmstead in Oklahoma where some of my family lived in the 1800s. Their living area, not unlike the caves in the Holy Land, was a room they had dug into the ground—an old cellar with a door and a chimney and an opening for daylight. A small building above ground served as the family's kitchen and dining room. In a part of the country that had few trees, underground living quarters made sense, particularly for people who could not afford to pay much for building materials—people who were just scraping by.

Living in caves in the Holy Land in ancient times, and still to the present, points to the humble station of those living in Nazareth and stands in stark contrast to the villas of nearby Sepphoris.

The Meaning of Nazareth

The name of this tiny village of Nazareth tells us something about the people living there and offers a clue to the identity of the child Mary would bear. Nazareth may come from the Hebrew *netzer,* which means "branch" or "shoot." Sometimes when a tree is chopped down, a shoot will grow from the stump, allowing a new tree to spring up where the old one has died. That shoot is called, in Hebrew, a *netzer.* Why would the people who founded this village have called it "the branch"?

Much of the Old Testament was written predicting, or in response to, the destruction of Israel. The northern half of the country was destroyed by the Assyrian Empire in 722 B.C. The southern half of the country, known as Judah, was destroyed by the Babylonian Empire in 587 or 586 B.C. The prophets, in speaking about the destruction and re-emergence of Israel, used the metaphor of Israel being like a tree that had been cut down, but which would sprout up once again. Israel would be led by a messianic figure called "the branch," so Isaiah 11:1-4, 6 says:

A shoot shall come up from the stump of Jesse
[Jesse, you remember, was King David's father],
    and a branch [*netzer*] shall grow out of his roots.
The Spirit of the LORD shall rest on him, . . .
His delight shall be in the fear of the LORD.
He shall not judge by what his eyes see,
    or decide by what his ears hear;
but with righteousness he shall judge the poor,
    and decide with equity for the meek of the earth; . . .

19

[And in those days] the wolf shall live with the lamb,
　　the leopard shall lie down with the kid,
　the calf and the lion and the fatling together,
　　and a little child shall lead them.

The *netzer* was a promise of hope. The word as used in Isaiah 11 pointed to the promise that, though Israel had been cut down like a felled tree, she would rise up once again. Fifty years after the destruction of Judah by the Babylonians, the Jewish people would return to the city of Jerusalem. Judah would rise up like a shoot. And the people hoped for the coming of the "branch" that the prophets foretold would lead the people—a messiah. (Jeremiah and Zechariah also use this same imagery, though they use a different word for "branch" than *netzer*.)

When the village founders named their village Nazareth they may have chosen this name as a way of expressing hope that God would once again restore Israel—that though Israel had been cut down by the Assyrians, the Babylonians, the Greeks, and then the Romans, a branch would come up from the stump. They may have chosen this name because, in the words of the prophet Isaiah, it was a sign that there are no hopeless causes with God. They may have chosen this name as a way of articulating their hope that one day the Messiah would come to Israel. It was as if they were saying, "We believe there is always hope. We believe God will deliver us. We believe the day will come when God will send a new king who will deliver us." Little did they know that the branch foretold in Isaiah, Jeremiah, and Zechariah would be a child who would grow up in their own village!

Why Nazareth?

So, with all that we've learned about this town and these people, the question is: Why here? Why did God choose this town of all places to find a young woman to bear the Christ? Why would

God choose this village, which was looked down upon by the people of Galilee ("Can anything good come out of Nazareth?") and which was of such low standing that it was not included in the lists of towns of Galilee? What does it tell us about God that this story did not take place in Sepphoris among the wealthy living in their luxury villas, but instead in Nazareth among working-class people, some of whom lived in caves? What does it tell you about whom God can use to accomplish his purposes, or where God's favor lies?

The setting of this story tells us that God looks for the meek and the humble to use for his greatest purposes. God chooses the least likely to accomplish his most important work. God chose a slave people to be his chosen people. God called the youngest of Jesse's seven sheepherding sons, David, to become Israel's greatest king. As Paul says to the Christians in Corinth, "God chose what is foolish in the world to shame the wise; God chose what is weak in the world to shame the strong; God chose what is low and despised in the world, things that are not, to reduce to nothing things that are" (1 Corinthians 1:27-28). James says it this way: "God opposes the proud, but gives grace to the humble" (James 4:6).

Mary

Let's look more closely at the woman God chose to be the mother of the Christ. She lived in this little, out-of-the-way town. She was likely uneducated and probably came from a poor family who may well have been servants in a household in Sepphoris. Perhaps they mopped the tile floors in a villa. It is obvious in any case that these were people without pretense. They were not people who believed the world revolved around them. They walked humbly with their God.

Mary was likely a girl of thirteen, although a more mature thirteen-year-old than we might expect. Young women married at that age in the ancient near East. We may find it strange today, but at a time when the average life expectancy was less than thirty-five years and most people did not go to school, girls were considered women when they had their first menstrual period, and they typically married shortly thereafter.

Mary was engaged to be married. According to custom, there would be a year-long legal engagement followed by a formal ceremony. Finally, she and her husband would consummate their marriage and begin having children. Every year it was expected that there would be another child. Women hoped and prayed that they might survive those births, one after the other over the course of their childbearing years.

Mature or not, Mary was no better prepared for the visit of an angel than any of us might be. Now, the word *angel* is a Greek word that means "messenger." We imagine these as winged creatures, but more likely Gabriel appeared to Mary as an ordinary man. There is no indication in the Scripture that she was terrified by his appearance, only by his message.

The Orthodox, as we saw, believe Mary was at the spring when Gabriel appeared to her. (The alternative name for the church built over the spring is the Church of St. Gabriel.) This tradition is traced back to the second century. Roman Catholics believe Mary was at her home when God's messenger appeared to her. Wherever he appeared, Gabriel's greeting was an interesting one. He said, "Hail, you who are full of grace! God is with you!" (See Luke 1:28.) Roman Catholics are familiar with a slightly different version of these words: "Hail, Mary, full of grace, the Lord is with thee!"

There has been a great deal of debate about the meaning of the phrase *full of grace.* Roman Catholic dogma states that this phrase, which is just one word in Greek, means that Mary was born in grace, without original sin. They speak of this as the immaculate conception of Mary—that she was conceived and born without sin. (Jesus also was born without sin and many Protestants mistakenly believe that the dogma of the "immaculate conception" refers to Jesus' conception.) Protestants tend to translate the word as "highly favored" and hold that God was showing Mary his favor, love, and grace. Protestants don't typically teach that Mary was conceived without sin and don't see in this phrase a warrant for teaching the immaculate conception of Mary. As a rule, Roman Catholics and Orthodox Christians have tended to exalt the role of Mary beyond what the biblical text may warrant based upon the traditions of the early church, while Protestants have tended to diminish Mary's role below what the text calls for. Regardless, it is clear that she was chosen by God as someone very, very special.

The words "full of grace" are a translation of only one word in Greek: *kecharitomene*. Do you see the underlined portion—the word *chari*? This word appears 170 times in the New Testament in one form or another. It is hugely important in the Christian faith, and it is central to the gospel. *Chari* is most often translated as "grace."

Kecharitomene is literally "one who has been filled with grace." So Gabriel addressed Mary as "full of grace." But what does *grace* mean? It's one of those words that we freely throw around and after awhile begins to lose its meaning.

In the New Testament, its meaning changes depending upon the context. Paul begins most of his letters saying, "Grace and peace to you." And he ends his letters with the words "May the grace of our Lord Jesus Christ be with you." We stand in God's grace, live by God's grace, are saved by God's grace, approach God in times of need asking for his grace. So what does *grace* mean? What is it?

Grace is God's kindness, his love, his care, God's work on our behalf, God's blessings, his gifts, his goodness, God's salvation. But it is more than that; it is these things when they are

> Grace is goodness that we don't deserve, kindness, salvation, forgiveness, blessing — all these things when they are pure gift.

undeserved. It is goodness that we don't deserve, kindness, salvation, forgiveness, blessing—all these things when they are pure gift. Further, the giving of grace—of love and blessing and kindness when we don't deserve them—has the power to change our lives.

These truths tell us something about God's character that has been made known in Jesus Christ. God is gracious. God is good, kind, loving, and compassionate, and desires good for his children. It is not something we deserve but is instead pure gift.

Grace is at the center of what God was doing in Christmas. The child to be born of Mary would embody and incarnate grace. His message would be a message of grace. His life would demonstrate grace to sinners, tax collectors, and prostitutes. They had been taught that there was no place for them in the synagogue, that God's judgment and wrath was upon them; Jesus devoted his life to showing them that it was God's love, mercy, and kindness that were offered to them. Jesus showed them grace.

Grace has power. When you show kindness, compassion, goodness, or love to someone who does not deserve it, the act of grace has the power to change hearts, to heal broken relationships, and to reconcile people and even nations. Grace changes the one who receives it, but it also changes the one who gives it.

In our story, Mary was indeed "full of grace," as the angel declared, but she was clearly confused, even frightened by it. Who was this strange man, and what did he mean that she was favored by God and that God was with her? Gabriel spoke soothingly,

Do not be afraid, Mary, for you have found favor with God. And now, you will conceive in your womb and bear a son, and you will name him Jesus. He will be great, and will be called the Son of the Most High, and the Lord God will give to him the throne of his ancestor David. He will reign over the house of Jacob forever, and of his kingdom there will be no end. (Luke 1:30-33)

Gabriel told Mary to name her son *Yeshua*. (*Jesus* comes from the Greek; but Mary would have heard Gabriel's words in Aramaic—and in that language his name was *Yeshua,* which means "God helps," "God saves," or "God delivers.") *Yeshua* was a common name in Mary's day: think of the common name, Joshua, which is variant of *Yeshua*. The name typically would have conjured up an image of a great warrior who would deliver God's people from their enemies. Jesus was indeed destined to be a deliverer; however, he would deliver the human race not by the power of a sword, but by the power of his cross, his resurrection, and the message he taught.

Gabriel told Mary that her child would be "great." Her son would teach his disciples one day what that word meant when he said that "whoever wishes to be great among you must be your servant" (Matthew 20:26). Gabriel also told Mary that her son would be called "the Son of the Most High." All Jewish children were considered sons and daughters of God. What may make Gabriel's statement unique was the presence of the article "the." Jesus would not be another son of the Most High, but he would be *the* Son of the Most High. Finally, Gabriel told Mary that her son was destined to be the long-awaited messianic king who would rule over the house of Jacob forever.

In celebrating Jesus' birth, Christians celebrate the birth of a deliverer, God's son, and the King of a kingdom that is eternal. His is a kingdom not defined by geography, but by the faith and devotion of all who call him Savior and Lord. Jesus would later describe this kingdom not so much as a place, but as a way of living. The citizens of God's kingdom love God and love their neighbor. They even love their enemies and pray for those who have wronged them. They forgive and act as peacemakers. In this kingdom, people follow the example of the good Samaritan; they clothe the naked, feed the hungry, give drink to the thirsty, and welcome the strangers. Christians believe that in knowing, loving, and serving Jesus as their king they find life, salvation, and hope.

The Virgin Birth

Mary's response to Gabriel's announcement was as practical as it was understandable. "How is this possible?" she asked. "I'm not married and I've never slept with a man." (The fact that she asked this question might tell us that she did not fully grasp what Gabriel had said about the identity of her son.)

Gabriel said to her, "God's Spirit will come upon you and the Most High will overshadow you. For this reason, your child will be holy and will be called the Son of God." (See Luke 1:35.)

This passage lays for us the foundation of the doctrine of the virgin birth, which might more accurately be called the virginal conception. Both Matthew and Luke report that Mary became pregnant in a supernatural way. They are not attempting to describe the biology of the conception and birth of Jesus. From a biological perspective, Mary could only supply half the required DNA, or Jesus would have been an exact clone of his mother. Gabriel's explanation of the virginal conception is not biological, but theological: "God's Spirit will come upon you and God will overshadow you." This could be taken to be sexual language, but that does not seem to be either Gabriel or Luke's intent. Their intent is to be clear that the biological reality of Mary's pregnancy was made possible by the direct action of God.

The church's doctrine of the virgin birth is meant to point to a union of humanity and divinity in Jesus. He was uniquely the Son of God, because God directly intervened to form him in the womb. The missing genetic material needed to form a child was from God. In a way unlike the Buddha, Mohammed, or any other religious figure revered by the masses, Jesus was the Son of God. He was both of Mary and of God.

In the Nicene Creed of A.D. 325, the church said that Jesus was "begotten" by the Father, and at the same time, by virtue of God's direct role in "begetting" Jesus, he was "very God of very God." God's essence, the "stuff" of God, was conjoined with human flesh. For this reason Jesus could say, "When you've seen me, you've seen the Father." Paul could write, "He is the image of the invisible God . . . in him all the fullness of God was pleased to dwell" (Colossians 1:15, 19).

Christians speak of the Incarnation when they speak of Jesus. This word means, in essence, "enfleshment." The idea is that something of the essence of God took on human flesh in the child in Mary's womb. In Jesus, divinity entered humanity; the Creator of the universe walked among us through the Son; and when he did, he came not as a conquering emperor living in the lap of luxury, but as a peasant, conceived out of wedlock, raised as the son of a carpenter in a village on "the other side of the tracks."

This idea of the virgin birth became a sticking point for Christians, particularly during the late nineteenth and early twentieth centuries. Viewing the world through the apparent certainty of science, with a belief that God might only do what modern scientists can prove, they asked, "How can we possibly believe in the virgin birth?" Some rejected Christianity altogether because of the difficulty of making sense of the virgin birth. Others, called "modernists," suggested that Mary and Joseph conceived Jesus in the usual way but that God had uniquely shaped their child and placed the Spirit within him and that the story of the virgin birth is less about describing how Jesus was conceived and more about making clear that he was uniquely God's son. (There were others, more progressive still, who rejected altogether the idea that Jesus was the unique Son of God.)

Some Christians responded by saying that the only way to believe Jesus was God's Son was if you affirmed the virginal conception of Jesus. They went on to say that if you didn't believe in the virginal conception, you couldn't call yourself a Christian. Others countered that the virginal conception is not mentioned by the apostle Paul or in the Gospels of Mark and John. They asked how, with such minimal emphasis on the idea in Scripture, this doctrine could possibly be a requirement for faith. After all, it seemed likely that many early Christians did not even know the story of how Jesus was conceived, so why should the doctrine of the virgin birth be seen as a requirement of the faith?

I understand the arguments of this latter group, and I am sympathetic to their desire to remove roadblocks that keep many thoughtful people from accepting the Christian faith. I also agree that many of the earliest Christians may not have been aware of the teaching concerning Jesus' virginal conception. Having said that, in a day and time when physicians artificially inseminate and when scientists are capable of cloning animals as well as human embryonic stem cells, belief in the virgin birth does not, to me, seem so difficult anymore. Is it really so hard to believe that the God who created the laws of biology and who designed our DNA could bring about a virginal conception?

Regardless of exactly how the virginal conception occurred, what is important to me in Matthew and Luke's moving stories is that they attempt to describe how Jesus was more than *a* son of God, but how he was uniquely *the* Son of God. They point to the fact that in Jesus, God's very essence had entered into human flesh. (The Greeks had a word for this; they spoke of God's *ousia*—the stuff of divinity.)

How exactly God brought about the conception of Jesus did not seem to be a terribly important point in Scripture, or else Mark, John, Paul, and the other disciples would have made direct reference to it. But while the exact *how* of the conception of Jesus was not seen as critical to these apostles, what the virginal conception points to was thought to be very important: namely, that "the child will be holy and will be called the Son of God."

Did Mary Want to Be Mary?

Thirteen-year-old Mary, standing by the spring of Nazareth and listening to the sound of water bubbling forth from the rock, heard the words of the messenger, and she tried desperately to take it all in. Would she really be the mother of the Messiah? She was to be pregnant, though out of wedlock. What would her family think? What would Joseph do? She asked Gabriel, "Tell me once more, how will this thing be?"

Yet, with her head spinning, filled with questions, uncertain what it all meant, Mary's response to Gabriel was simple and profound. She did not need to understand fully. She simply said, "Here am I, the servant of the Lord; let it be with me according to your word" (Luke 1:38).

Mary said, "Yes," despite knowing that, according to the law, young women who were legally engaged but found to be pregnant by someone other than their betrothed were to be stoned to death. (See Deuteronomy 22:23-24.) She said, "Yes," despite knowing that some women died in childbirth. She said, "Yes," despite knowing that it would mean the end of the dreams she had for her wedding day, and it would likely lead to Joseph calling off the marriage. She said, "Yes," despite knowing that she might be an unwed mother with child.

Protestants have long reacted to what they perceive as an overemphasis on Mary within Roman Catholicism. We hear Roman Catholics refer to Mary as the "Queen of Heaven" and we chafe a bit. We've reacted by downplaying Mary and minimizing the role she played in God's plan.

However, it is important to stop and recognize that, aside from Jesus himself, no other human being played so crucial a role in the salvation of the human race as Mary. The redemption of humanity, and God's plans to step into our world, all hinged upon what Mary would say to Gabriel, the messenger.

Her assent set in motion the mystery of the Incarnation. As a consequence of her willingness, Mary's own body knit together the Messiah. It was her blood that carried nutrients to the child. It was her tender words, spoken and sung as mothers do to the children in their wombs, that quieted and comforted him. For nine months, divinity resided within her womb. No one before or since has had such intimate union with God. An ancient Christian hymn captures Mary's role in our salvation when it says, "He whom the entire universe could not contain was contained within your womb." The early church called her *Theotokos*—the one who gives birth to God—as a way of capturing both the identity of her son and the importance of her role in this story.

When Mary finally gave birth to Jesus and suckled him, the Son of God was fed and sustained by the milk from her breasts. She tenderly held him. She changed his diapers and bathed him and sang him to sleep. She taught him and instilled in him faith in his heavenly Father. She feared for him, cried for him, and, more than anything, loved him. And, thirty-three years after his birth, she stood by and wept as her son died on a Roman cross.

These are deep, profound thoughts, and we have only begun to explore them. For while this part of the story is Mary's, we find ourselves in the story too. Writing in a blog for *The Christian Century* a few years ago, Christian Coon told the story of a children's Christmas pageant at the church where he was pastor. Dozens of children had come for the chance to sing and dance and dress up as wise men and shepherds, as sheep, donkeys, and camels. None of the boys were fighting over the chance to play Joseph, because he didn't get any lines. But then the director asked, "Now, who wants to be Mary?"

Hands shot up and eyes danced as all the little girls jumped up and down. Every one of them wanted to be Mary. Hers was the starring role![1]

But then Coon asked this question: "Do you think Mary wanted to be Mary?" What do you think? Knowing the scandal and potential punishment for conception outside of wedlock, knowing that her hopes and dreams for a traditional wedding would come to an end, do you think Mary wanted to be Mary? Yet, with heart pounding, with uncertainty, fear, and confusion, Mary's response was clear: "Here am I, the servant of the Lord."

As we consider that moment of decision for Mary, we see in her a witness and an example of how we are meant to live. Her mission reminds us that God's call is sometimes difficult. It may lead us to set aside our own plans. It may mean giving up hopes and dreams we have cherished for a lifetime. It may mean risks. It may be frightening.

Sometimes God asks us to be with people we don't want to be with, to go to places we don't want to go to, and to do things we don't want to do. This is part of what Mary's story teaches us. Mary is twice said to be favored by God, and yet God's favor meant not a life of bliss, but a life of risk. It must have been hard to imagine that this was what it meant to be favored by God.

Knowing how Mary responded to God's request, we are inspired, with her, to say, "Here am I, the servant of the Lord; let it be with me according to your word."

As we prepare our hearts for Christmas, we remember the little town of Nazareth and God's choice of a young woman from this humble village through whom he would do his greatest work. This season brings us an invitation as surely as Gabriel brought Mary an invitation. Part of the invitation of Advent, the season leading up to Christmas, is to offer ourselves wholly to God just as Mary did. Christmas is not about how much you buy or what you eat or whom you visit. It is about your willingness to say, with Mary, "Here am I, Lord. Use me according to your will."

Reflection
An Angel Named Gabriel

What do you think about angels? A *Washington Times* poll found that half of all Americans believe in them. The other half were not so sure. If we're talking about little babies with wings flitting about shooting arrows into the hearts of lovers, I'm not biting. If we're thinking John Travolta with giant wings as he portrayed the archangel Michael in a 1996 film, I'm still saying, "Nope." Clarence talking poor George Bailey off the bridge in *It's a Wonderful Life* starts to get a little closer to the angels of the Scriptures, but skip the part about him earning his wings.

When we read about angels in Scripture it is important to remember that the word *angel* simply means "messenger." Angels typically appear simply as people—no wings, just people. Sometimes their attire is majestic or glorious, but usually they're just strangers with a word from God. Sometimes they come in visions. But sometimes they come in the flesh. The writer of Hebrews notes that some Christians in his day, as they welcomed strangers, had welcomed angels without knowing it.

In our Scripture, Mary was perplexed by Gabriel's words but not by his appearance; hence he appeared as a stranger who told Mary a word about God's will for her life and who invited her to be open and willing to answer God's call.

To my knowledge I've never met the heavenly kind of angel. But there have been many people whose messages changed my life. When I was fourteen years old, a man named Harold Thorson knocked on my door. He spoke with an electrolarynx (a device that looks like a microphone pressed to the throat, to allow speech for those whose larynx has been removed). He was going door to door in my neighborhood, inviting people to church. Though I did not believe in God I was moved by this man's visit and started attending church, and my life was forever changed. While in college I was selling women's shoes in a department store. Belinda came in to try on shoes, but before she left she also invited my wife and me to visit the Methodist church she attended. We'd been looking for a church. Her invitation, and our visit to her church, led to a call to be a part of renewing The United Methodist Church. How different my life would have been had Harold Thorson not gone visiting door to door, or Belinda not listened to the nudge in her heart to invite me to her church.

There have been a thousand more messengers since then. I think of the pastors whose preaching I heard week after week, and how God spoke to me through them. My professors at college and seminary, too. My wife has certainly been a messenger from God for me on countless occasions. And members of the church I serve, such as Nancy, whose persistent invitations led me to visit southern Africa years ago, a visit that would have a profound impact upon my ministry.

Which leads me to a question for you: Do you take the time, do you pay attention to what's happening around you, and do you listen so that you don't miss God's angels when they come speaking to you?

Today many of us are so busy, so preoccupied, or in such a hurry that there is no time to listen to how God may be trying to speak to us. Imagine if Gabriel had approached Mary while she was fetching water and she had said, "I'm sorry, I'm really busy right now. Do you think you could come back later?" Or if she had dismissed him as a crackpot when he tried to tell her about God's plans for her life. And yet this is precisely the response many of us would have in our busy and pre-occupied lives today.

God speaks through Scripture, through the still small voice of the Holy Spirit, but God also speaks through people (and occasionally heavenly messengers who look like them). Pay attention! Listen, lest you miss out on God's purposes for your life.

Lord, thank you for the people through whom you have spoken to me. Help me to pay attention and to listen for your voice through those you send. Speak, Lord; your servant is listening. Amen.

From *The Journey: A Season of Reflections.* Abingdon Press, 2011.

Travel Notes

Sepphoris and Nazareth

Sepphoris is an old Roman city just four miles from the smaller town of Nazareth. At the time of Jesus' birth, Sepphoris was a bustling city with a population of thousands. It was a center of culture, both Hebrew and Greek, and many townspeople of the much more modest Nazareth worked in Sepphoris.

In the ruins of Sepphoris are traces of its former glory. You can still see outlines of luxurious homes and their colorful mosaic floors, the most famous of which is the "Madonna of the Galilee." (The woman in the mosaic is not believed to be Mary.) From these ruins, you can look down to the small village of Nazareth, where Mary and her family lived.

An easy three-mile walk brings you to Mary's hometown. Today, 72,000 people live in the city of Nazareth, and 210,000 live along the hillsides of greater Nazareth. But in Jesus' day, Nazareth was a tiny village of just a few hundred.

The Orthodox Church of the Annunciation is a beautiful structure built over the spring that originally brought settlers to Nazareth. In his ministry Jesus referred to "living water," and beneath the church we can still see the spring of living water that he may have envisioned as he said those words.

Travel Photos

Adam in Nazareth

Sepphoris

Nazareth

Church of the Annunciation, Nazareth

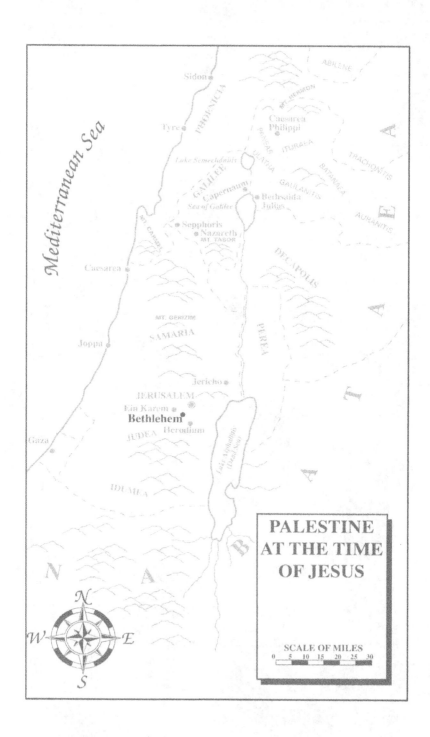

Mediterranean Sea

Sidon

Tyre

PHOENICIA

ABILENE

MT. HERMON

Caesarea
Philippi

PANEAS ITURAEA

Lake Semechonitis

ULATHA

GALILEE

Capernaum
Sea of Galilee

Bethsaida
Julias

GAULANITIS

BATANEA

TRACHONITIS

AURANITIS

Sepphoris
Nazareth
MT. TABOR

DECAPOLIS

Caesarea

MT. CARMEL

MT. GERIZIM

SAMARIA

PEREA

Joppa

Jericho

JERUSALEM

Ein Karem
Bethlehem
Herodium

JUDEA

Lake Asphaltitis
(Dead Sea)

Gaza

IDUMEA

N A B A T

**PALESTINE
AT THE TIME
OF JESUS**

N

W   E

S

SCALE OF MILES

0   5   10   15   20   25   30

2. Joseph of Bethlehem

Now the birth of Jesus the Messiah took place this way. When his mother Mary had been engaged to Joseph, but before they lived together, she was found to be with child from the Holy Spirit. Her husband Joseph, being a righteous man and unwilling to expose her to public disgrace, planned to dismiss her quietly. But just when he had resolved to do this, an angel of the Lord appeared to him in a dream and said, "Joseph, son of David, do not be afraid to take Mary as your wife, for the child conceived in her is from the Holy Spirit. She will bear a son, and you are to name him Jesus, for he will save his people from their sins." All this took place to fulfill what had been spoken by the Lord through the prophet: "Look, the virgin shall conceive and bear a son, and they shall name him Emmanuel," which means, "God is with us." When Joseph awoke from sleep, he did as the angel of the Lord commanded him; he took her as his wife.

(Matthew 1:18-24)

O Little Town of Bethlehem

As TAKEN ABACK AS MARY WAS by the visit of the angel and by the enormity of the choice laid before her, there was someone else who was surely just as shocked. We turn our attention now to the other half of the human equation: Mary's fiancé, Joseph, a good and decent man who learned that his young bride-to-be was with child and who knew that he was not the father.

Mary's story is told in the Gospel of Luke, Joseph's in the Gospel of Matthew. Although both accounts describe the events leading up to the birth of Jesus, Matthew and Luke's tellings of these stories have striking differences. Luke's begins in Nazareth with Mary. Matthew's story is set in Bethlehem. People tend to merge these accounts, which makes for a less-than-accurate view of what took place.

We usually assume that Mary and Joseph both lived in Nazareth when Mary discovered she was pregnant. Further, we assume Joseph was in Nazareth when Mary told him the news that she was with child. Following that, they were married; the couple then traveled to Bethlehem only after the census decreed by the Romans required them to do so, just before the birth of Jesus.

If you read Matthew by itself, though, you find that Nazareth is not mentioned until Chapter 2, verse 23, by which time Jesus was likely at least two years old. In Matthew's Gospel, Bethlehem appears to be Joseph's hometown. Luke 2:3 would seem to corroborate this when it notes that, with the census, "All went to their own towns to be registered." This would imply that Joseph's "own town" was Bethlehem. (You may object that if Bethlehem was Joseph's hometown, why did Mary give birth in a stable rather than in Joseph's family's home? But for the answer to that question, you'll have to wait until Chapter 4!)

Since Nazareth was certainly Mary's hometown, Joseph and Mary's engagement was most likely long-distance, arranged by their respective families in Bethlehem and Nazareth. Further evidence that Bethlehem was Joseph's hometown may come in the story we'll explore shortly: Mary's visit to her cousin Elizabeth (Luke 1:39-56). The traditional location of Elizabeth and Zechariah's home is called Ein Karem, only four miles from Bethlehem. So, immediately upon discovering she was pregnant, Mary traveled nine days south to a town four miles from Bethlehem, where she would spend the next three months.

If, as I am suggesting, Joseph's hometown was Bethlehem, then it would have been during this time that Joseph visited Mary and learned that his betrothed was pregnant. It would have been during this time, these first three months of Mary's pregnancy, that Joseph would have had his own "annunciation" by means of a dream. Following those events, he would have taken Mary back to Nazareth, where the couple was married and began their life together until forced to return to Bethlehem for the census.

Bethlehem in Joseph's day was a village of perhaps five hundred to a thousand people. It was a two-hour walk—six miles—from Jerusalem. Bethlehem means "House of Bread." It was home to laborers and sheepherders, but it was also home to farmers who grew wheat and barley and likely to millers and bakers—hence the name, "House of Bread." We can surmise that bread was baked there and then probably delivered to customers in Jerusalem.

Unlike Nazareth, which was virtually unknown, Bethlehem was a well-known town. Though not large, it was known as the place where Rachel had died giving birth to Benjamin. Rachel's husband, Jacob, buried her near this town and built a monument to her that stood for hundreds of years. Bethlehem was also the setting of the Book of Ruth. Ruth's great-grandson was a child named David, a shepherd boy whom Samuel the prophet anointed to be king over Israel. Before assuming the throne, while still a boy, David slew the giant, Goliath, with just a sling-shot and a few smooth stones.

Bethlehem became associated with David, the great king. The city became known (along with Jerusalem) as "the City of David." Several hundred years after the time of David, Micah the prophet foretold the day when a new king would come from Bethlehem: "But you, O Bethlehem of Ephrathah, / who are one of the little clans of Judah, / from you shall come forth for me / one who is to rule in Israel, / whose origin is from of old, / from ancient days" (Micah 5:2, also quoted in Matthew 2:6). This passage was understood to foretell the day another king, like David, would reign over God's people—a king who would be a shepherd to God's people.

Growing up in Bethlehem, Joseph would have known those words of Micah. The boy children of Bethlehem likely grew up pretending to be David slaying Goliath, or David defeating the Philistines, or David the great king of Israel. And they would have grown up learning that one day the Messiah would come from their midst. Yet it should be noted that even in the days of Joseph, the town of Bethlehem was primarily a working-class town of people who served the needs of those with resources in Jerusalem. Once more we find that God demonstrates a propensity to choose and use people who live in relative obscurity and whose lives and spirits reflect true humility.

Joseph the Carpenter

It is this humility that stands out when considering Joseph and his story. He doesn't speak a single word in the New Testament. He is mentioned only a handful of times in the Bible. The final time we hear of Joseph, Jesus is twelve years old. Joseph is mentioned briefly after this in reference to being Jesus' father, but we do not know whether he was still alive at that time.

So little is known about Joseph that by the beginning of the second century, Christians began to develop traditions about him—traditions that are not likely historically accurate, although we cannot be sure. They began to teach that Joseph was an elderly widower when he married Mary; one source says he was 93 at the time and lived to be 111, dying when Jesus was 18. This tradition seemed to have developed as a way of asserting that a kind elderly gentleman took Mary in to care for her, and since he was more like a grandfather than a husband, the marriage was never consummated and Mary remained a virgin throughout her life. This picture of Joseph also provided one possible explanation for the brothers and sisters of Jesus mentioned in Matthew 13:55-56 and elsewhere: they could have been Joseph's children by a deceased wife. (Roman Catholics, for whom the doctrine of the perpetual virginity of Mary is important, will also point out that "brothers and sisters" in the Gospels can also mean cousins or close family members.)

This idea that Joseph was elderly is represented in a good deal of art from the Orthodox and Roman Catholic traditions, where Joseph is often portrayed as an older man. Most Protestants who regard the second-century traditions that developed about Joseph as spurious assume that Joseph was likely the age of any other young man getting married at the time—around fourteen or fifteen. So, Protestant portrayals tend to show Joseph as a young man. (As an aside, take a look at your nativity set and see if your Joseph is portrayed as an older man or a young man; if he is older the artist likely came from a Roman Catholic or Eastern Orthodox tradition.)

We do know from Mark 6:3 that Joseph was a carpenter. The Greek word used to describe him in the New Testament is *tekton,* which can mean woodworker, craftsman, and possibly stonemason. You'll recognize *tekton* as part of the word "architect." An *arch-tekton* was a "master-builder," just as an "archangel" was a lead angel. Yet Joseph was not an *arch-tekton,* only a *tekton*—not a master builder, but simply a humble woodworker.

In Israel very few homes are built of wood. Most in Joseph's day were made of stone. Doors and roofs would have been constructed by men like Joseph. He may also have built and repaired farming tools; *tektons* played this important role in farming villages. Woodworking tools changed little through the centuries, so Joseph's tools may well have been like the tools used by carpenters and woodworkers until the advent of modern power tools.

When I think of Joseph, the earthly father of Jesus, I think of my own great-grandfather, Joseph Lorson. He died when I was just a boy, but I can still picture him sitting in the front room of my grandparents' home. He was a giant of a man, with huge hands. He, too, was a carpenter. He was a man of few words but as honest as the day is long. My dad tells me he was patient and persistent when it came to his work and very careful with the money he earned. He was a "salt of the earth" kind of man who worked with his hands. This is how I picture Joseph, the earthly father of Jesus.

Some years ago, while preparing to preach a sermon on Joseph, I interviewed a team of carpenters on a construction site. I asked these guys, based on what they knew of carpenters, what they thought Joseph would have been like and why they thought God chose Joseph to be the earthly father of Jesus. Their responses were quite moving. They thought Joseph would have been a man who liked to work with his hands, one who put in a hard day's work and took pride in what he had done. They imagined him as someone who enjoyed working outdoors or in his shop and who understood the importance of doing something right the first time. Those who had sons could also picture Joseph teaching his trade to Jesus as his son grew up.

Humble, hardworking, honest, a craftsman, a person who took pride in his work—these are a few of the images I have in my mind when I think of Joseph the carpenter.

Joseph Learns His Betrothed Is Pregnant

When we meet Joseph in Matthew's Gospel, he had just learned that his young betrothed was pregnant. Mary and Joseph, as we said in the previous chapter, were formally engaged through a legally binding ceremony. In a sense, they were already married; all that was left was the official ceremony, the consummation of the marriage, the honeymoon, and the move to Joseph's home, which typically happened a year after the betrothal. It was during this in-between time that Joseph found out Mary was pregnant.

Matthew tells us that Mary "was found to be with child from the Holy Spirit. Her husband Joseph, being a righteous man and unwilling to expose her to public disgrace, planned to dismiss her quietly" (1:18-19). There's a lot that's not said in this verse. Let's try to fill in the missing information.

Joseph must not have believed the story Mary told about the angel and the virginal conception; if he had believed it, he would not have been looking for a way to break off the engagement. The only logical explanation was that Mary had been unfaithful to him.

It is not hard to imagine what Joseph felt upon learning of Mary's apparent unfaithfulness. He would be devastated by this news. How could Mary do this? Joseph likely felt betrayed, dishonored, humiliated, and hurt by Mary and the other man. As Mary tried to explain how she came to be with child, I imagine Joseph's hurt giving way to anger. Joseph's whole world would have been shaken by this news from Mary. His trust had been violated. In his anger he may have reminded Mary that the law commanded that women who were adulterous were to be put to death. If he told others what he knew, she would die. As noted earlier, Joseph probably learned from Mary that she was pregnant while she was staying at the home of Zechariah and Elizabeth. Bethlehem was only a few miles away, and Joseph likely had come to call upon Mary there. It's easy to imagine that Joseph, upon learning this news, left Elizabeth's home, heartbroken and unwilling to speak to Mary. I can see Mary weeping as he walked away.

At some point during Joseph's ninety-minute walk back to Bethlehem, his anger must have given way to concern for Mary's life. If he told others what had happened, that Mary was pregnant with another man's child, Mary would be stoned to death. Mary's life was in his hands. Joseph was hurt, but he did not want to see Mary die. He began to develop a plan to break off the engagement formally and legally, but to do so without explaining the reason why.

Joseph knew that after he ended the engagement, everyone would soon discover that Mary was pregnant. They would naturally assume that Joseph was the father and that he had slept with her while she was in Ein Karem, then broken off the engagement. The shame would be his, not Mary's. Mary's life would be spared, and she would have the pity of her family. Mary's family would keep the dowry that had already been paid, and Joseph would provide the agreed-upon additional dowry that would have been provided at his wedding. He would also provide for the child and, if Mary's father insisted, he could be required to take her as his wife.

Joseph was willing to do all this because he was a "righteous man." Note that Joseph's righteousness came not from seeking to obey the law, which was clear at this point—Mary should have been stoned to death if Joseph really believed she'd been unfaithful. It was not his obedience to the law, nor his pursuit of justice, that defined Joseph's righteousness. Instead, it was Joseph's compassion and mercy that led Matthew to call him righteous.

48

Wrestling With Our Darkest Moments

Another lesson for our lives is implied in Joseph's story on that day when he discovered Mary was pregnant. As Joseph heard the news and then began his journey back to Bethlehem, he might well have been convinced that this was the worst day of his life. I suspect most of us would have felt that same way. This journey was not one Joseph had anticipated. It was not a journey he wanted to take. The road back felt, literally, like hell.

Have you ever taken a journey like that—a journey you felt was the worst of your life? Have you felt that your hopes and dreams had been crushed and you simply didn't want to go on? This is what Joseph must have been feeling that day.

Here's what I want you to notice: At that very moment when Joseph felt at his lowest, God was at work in Mary's womb, doing the greatest thing God had done since the creation of the human race. God was orchestrating the birth of the Savior. God was also inviting Joseph to play a critical part in this plan. Something amazing was about to happen, but Joseph could not see this yet.

In my life God has always taken the pain, the disappointment, the heartache and used it in profound ways that I could only see and understand in hindsight. Today when I face moments of profound disappointment, and journeys that I don't want to take, I turn them over to God and invite him to, in the words of the apostle Paul, make "all things work together for good for those who love God, and are called according to his purpose" (Romans 8:28).

When life gets hard and even painful, we would do well to remember Joseph. Just as it all seems to be going wrong, it could be then that God is doing something remarkable that you or I simply cannot see yet. God takes our disappointments, heartache, and pain and uses them in profound ways. If Joseph had simply walked away that day, leaving Mary as a single mom to raise the child she was carrying, imagine what blessings he would have missed and how different the Gospel story may have been. It's a reminder to us to be cautious about walking away from disappointing situations.

That night Joseph went to sleep; and, as he slept, he had a dream that was almost like a vision. He saw a messenger of God in his dream—an angel. "Joseph," the messenger said, "do not be afraid to take Mary as your wife, for the child conceived in her is from the Holy Spirit. She will bear a son, and you are to name him Jesus, for he will save his people from their sins" (Matthew 1:20-21).

The effect of that dream on Joseph was profound. He woke up the next morning, returned to Ein Karem, and told Mary of his dream. He told her that he believed her. He told her that he would marry her and that he would raise the child as his own. It is likely that shortly after this, Mary and Joseph made their way to Nazareth, hastily arranging the wedding ceremony.

O Come, O Come, Emmanuel

Let's return to Matthew's account of the virginal conception and the annunciation to Joseph concerning this conception: "All this took place to fulfill what had been spoken by the Lord through the prophet: 'Look, the virgin shall conceive and bear a son, and they shall name him Emmanuel,' which means 'God is with us'" (Matthew 1:22-23). These words are Matthew's editorial comment on the story.

Matthew is quoting the prophet Isaiah. You have undoubtedly heard the prophecy before. It is an integral and compelling part of the Nativity story. It is found in Isaiah 7:14, and it was written about 735 years before Jesus was born. I'd like to take a moment to consider this passage, for it illustrates how early Christians read the Scriptures that today we call the Old Testament.

In some ways, like the discussion in the last chapter of the virgin birth, this verse from Isaiah has been debated over the years.

Let's begin by recognizing that the promise that a "virgin shall conceive, and bear a son" (KJV) was probably not understood by Isaiah to be about a child to be born seven hundred years into the future, but instead about Isaiah's own son. Most Christians are unfamiliar with the actual context of the prophecy in Isaiah. You might want to get your Bible out for this. Turn to Isaiah 7:1-16.

When Isaiah penned his prophecy about a virgin conceiving and bearing a child, he was living within the walls of the city of Jerusalem. Beyond the walls, two armies had laid siege to the city—the army of the Kingdom of Israel (Jerusalem was, at this time, the capital of the Kingdom of Judah) and the army of the Kingdom of Aram (modern-day Syria). The people of Jerusalem were terrified, as was Judah's king, Ahaz. But God gave Isaiah a word of hope for King Ahaz: Judah would be spared, and Israel and Aram would be defeated by their foes, the Assyrians. God gave Ahaz a sign that this would come to pass:

> Therefore the Lord himself will give you a sign. Look, the young woman is with child and shall bear a son, and shall name him Immanuel. He shall eat curds and honey by the time he knows how to refuse the evil and choose the good. For before the child knows how to refuse the evil and choose the good, the land before whose two kings you are in dread will be deserted. (Isaiah 7:14-16)

Note that the New Revised Standard Version (NRSV) of Isaiah 7:14 quoted here indicates that it was a "young woman," not a virgin, who would conceive and bear a child. The Hebrew word can be translated as either virgin or young woman. The NRSV chose "young woman" to make clear that the woman in question here was Isaiah's own wife or fiancée. In Chapter 8,

Isaiah lies with his wife and she conceives and has a child, and before the child was thirteen (the age a child was considered an adult and thus held accountable for knowing right from wrong), the Assyrians had destroyed both the kingdoms of Aram and Israel just as Isaiah had foretold. Immanuel was the name given to Isaiah's own son, because his birth and life were a reminder of God's promise to be with, and to deliver, God's people.

The child Isaiah prophesied concerning was a sign, a visible reminder of God's concern for and ultimate protection of his people. He embodied the hope that God had not abandoned Jerusalem.

If the child Isaiah prophesied about was his own son, or some other child born in Isaiah's day, why did Matthew say that Jesus' conception and birth fulfilled Isaiah 7:14? Some scholars assume Matthew was either ignorant of the original context of Isaiah 7:14, or that he was intentionally lifting a passage from Hebrew Scripture and using it to mean something it did not originally mean. I don't think this was the case. Matthew was not confused nor was he misinterpreting Isaiah. When Matthew quoted this verse from Isaiah, I think he was saying, "Jesus, like that first Immanuel, was a sign sent by God that you might know God is with you, that you might know he will never leave you, that you might know he will deliver you! What happened in the days of Isaiah is happening again!"

Jesus, in a way that the first Immanuel could not, incarnated the presence and love of the God who rules over the entire universe. Unlike Isaiah's child, Jesus was the Son of God, wrapped in human flesh so the invisible was made visible, born in a stable so we might know that we are not alone. This new Immanuel was God's way of assuring humanity that no matter how dark your circumstances, no matter how afraid you might be, no matter what is happening in your life or in the world around you, God is always with you. Jesus is the visible sign from God that God is with us.

We too are called to be signs of Immanuel — of God's presence in the world — and to be visible reminders of hope.

But the Immanuel "prophecy" may also say something about what God expects of Jesus' followers. Isaiah's son was Immanuel for his generation—a visible reminder of God's promise to be with us. Jesus, in a much more profound way, is Immanuel to every generation since his birth—a visible reminder that God is with us. But in a sense, as Christ's followers, we too are called to incarnate God's presence in the world. We too are called to be signs of Immanuel—of God's presence in the world—and to be visible reminders of hope.

All of us know people who are walking through tough times, who feel besieged in one way or another. How will those people know that God is with them, that they are not alone, if we don't embody God's love and presence to them? We are called to show by our actions the love of Christ. We are called to act as a reminder that "God is with you," to come alongside someone and say, "Listen, I am here to remind you that God has not forgotten you."

I recently spoke to a couple who had been through a series of devastating and frightening circumstances: the death of a family member, the loss of jobs, and a sickness that left one of them debilitated. In the midst of all this, both of their cars quit running. The couple told me that what had saved them in those tough times was the presence of their fellow church members who visited them, called upon them, encouraged them, took up an offering for them, helped them, and gave them hope. These church members were their Immanuel.

When I visit church members in the hospital, I always pray as I'm walking in that I might embody the presence of God for the person I am visiting. I pray, "God, please help me to be a physical reminder to this person that you are with them." In those moments, I have the opportunity be a physical reminder of Immanuel. This is God's call for us all—to be Immanuel for others.

Several years ago my wife, my children, and I, along with several other families, drove to Bay St. Louis, Mississippi, to serve alongside the people who were affected by Hurricane Katrina. We mucked out houses and tore out moldy sheet rock and insulation from homes that had been completely submerged in the floods. At one home, we finished our work as the sun was setting. The family we were serving came out to meet us on the driveway to thank us. Their matriarch described how it felt to be in the attic as the floodwaters rose and how terrified she was. She talked about how it felt to lose everything. When she had finished speaking, I looked at her and said, "We just want you to know the reason we came was to be a visible sign that God has not forgotten you. We felt God sent us to remind you that God is with you."

Do you know someone who has lost a loved one, who has been out of work for some time, who is facing physical illness, who has been divorced or is walking through some other dark place? How might you be a modern-day Immanuel to that person—a physical reminder of God's presence and love? Jesus, in a way no one else could, embodied or incarnated God's presence. But we, as his followers, can seek to embody his presence for others.

Joseph, the Earthly Father of Jesus

From the time my children were born, I would pray that God would help me to love them with his love. I prayed that I could, as their earthly father, help them by my actions to see and know their Heavenly Father. I sought to teach them what God was like, both by my actions and by my words. In so many ways I failed at this, but this was my prayer and hope.

While we don't read it explicitly in the Gospels, we can infer from the life and teachings of Jesus the profound impact Joseph had on Jesus' faith. When Jesus looked for a metaphor to describe his relationship—and ours—to God, his primary form of addressing God was *Abba*—the Aramaic word for Papa. It is likely that even as a boy Jesus saw in Joseph a picture of the love and character of God.

We see evidence of this throughout Jesus' teachings. We see it in the parable of the prodigal son, where Jesus likened God to a father who showed mercy to a son who had squandered his inheritance, while showing patience with his older son who judged the younger. Could this parable be a reflection of Jesus' own experience of Joseph's mercy and love? In what other ways might Joseph's heart, character, and faith have shaped Jesus' faith and the man he would become?

It appears from reading the Gospels that by the time Jesus was a man and had begun his public ministry Joseph was no longer living. As I noted previously, Joseph was never mentioned as being present after Jesus was twelve years old, though Joseph was clearly remembered by people when Jesus began his public ministry. (See John 6:42 and Matthew 13:55.)

Herod and Joseph: A Contrast in Character

Assuming Joseph was a young man when Jesus was conceived, one king had ruled over Judea during Joseph's entire life: Herod "the Great." Herod ruled Judea, with the blessing and help of the Romans, for thirty-three years, from 37 B.C. to 4 B.C. Much has been written about Herod's life that can be read elsewhere. I only want to mention a few facts about Herod, particularly his activity near Bethlehem, as a way of pointing out the difference between Herod the king and Joseph the carpenter.

It is generally agreed that Herod desperately wanted the praise, admiration, and love of others. He hoped to be seen as the messianic king the prophets foretold, even if he did not meet the criteria found in the prophets. Herod hoped to restore the greatness of the Jewish kingdom. Herod also loved the wealth and power that went with being king. He was adept at amassing wealth from the people and maintaining a firm grip on power. Unlike Jesus and Joseph, Herod had nothing of the servant's heart. For Herod, greatness was found not in servanthood but in affirmation and acknowledgment, and in a life of ease and luxury.

Herod seems constantly to have been working to prove his own greatness to others (and perhaps to himself) and to secure his place in history. Part of this effort took the form of massive building projects. Herod rebuilt the Temple in Jerusalem on a grand scale, exceeding the splendor of the original Temple built by Solomon. He built cities and seaports, fortresses and palaces. Evidence of his reign can be seen in ruins throughout the land of Israel and Palestine.

One of the most interesting of Herod's building projects was called the *Herodium* (sometimes *Herodion*)—yes, Herod named it after himself! The *Herodium* was a man-made mountain—Herod's version of a pyramid—but unlike the Egyptian pyramids that were used only to bury the dead, Herod's pyramid would serve as his winter palace and fortress, though he would ultimately be buried there as well.

This mountain fortress rose four hundred feet in the air, fifty feet taller than the Great Pyramid at Giza. At the base Herod built villas for his friends and a huge pond and pool for their enjoyment (remember, this was the desert—it was quite a sight to see). Midway up his mountain was a theater with seating for up to nine hundred people. At the top was a palace "fit for a king." There were Roman baths, a large central hall, and bedrooms.

The connection to Joseph is simply this: Herod's palace was located adjacent to Bethlehem. It could be seen from nearly anywhere in Bethlehem, and the people of Bethlehem undoubtedly

Herod's massive Herodium, as seen from Bethlehem

marveled as they watched it built. Some of the residents of Bethlehem likely were conscripted to help build Herod's monument to his own greatness. And this building offers us a study in contrasts. In Chapter 4 we'll devote a bit more space to examining the contrast between Herod and Jesus, but here I'm struck by a particular contrast between Herod and Joseph.

Herod was a builder on a massive scale; Joseph was a simple carpenter. Herod lived a kind of prodigal and wanton lifestyle, always pursuing the affirmation of others; Joseph lived a life of simplicity and humility, seeking primarily to please God.

From the splendor of this hilltop palace, Herod the Great could look down at a tiny part of the kingdom he ruled: that hardscrabble little town of Bethlehem, where lived a family of humble carpenters. In contrast to Herod, who wanted so desperately to make an immortal mark, Joseph had no such aspirations but did in fact change the world. Joseph's role as the earthly father of Jesus shaped Jesus' life, ministry, and teachings and, through them, shaped all who follow Jesus.

The ruins of Herod's monuments stand as testimony to a man who was remembered, within a few short months of his death, for his self-centeredness, self-indulgence, and arrogance. Joseph, on the other hand, left no monuments. We don't have a single recorded word he spoke. His story reminds us that life is not about affirmation, wealth, or power, but about humbly serving God and others. Joseph is the patron saint of those who give themselves to God, who live a costly faith and never receive, nor expect, any credit.

No one ever prays, "Hail, Joseph, full of grace. The Lord is with thee." Joseph doesn't have a book of the New Testament named for him. He has no honorific title. None of his words are preserved in Scripture, and he is only mentioned a handful of times in the Bible. But perhaps this is precisely the lesson we're meant to learn from Joseph. He was a simple, humble man who did what God asked.

Jesus likely learned from Joseph something he taught his disciples. "Be careful not to do your acts of righteousness to be seen by others," he said, "so that you get credit in their eyes. If you do you will have received your reward. Instead, do your acts of righteousness in secret—your Father will see and will reward you." (See Luke 6:1-6.) Joseph modeled what Jesus later taught his disciples: "The one who would be great among you, must first be your servant." (See Matthew 20:26-27.)

When we look at Joseph, we are meant to see God's call to humble service and obedience. Most of us want to be like Joseph—to serve God and others and to do so selflessly and without regard for recognition and affirmation. Yet there is enough of Herod in us that sometimes we get discouraged because nobody seems to notice us.

Joseph models for us how to serve without expectation of reward. He had the most important job ever given to a man up to that point. His was the task of raising Jesus and teaching him how to be a man. He did this without recognition, without the praise of others, solely because God called him in a dream to care for God's Son.

Allow me to ask you the question I've asked myself many times: Who will you choose to be? Will you be Herod, who spent his life seeking to win the praise of others and pursuing wealth, power, and material possessions, and who by his actions seemed to say, "Here I am, notice me!"? Or will you be Joseph, who was a humble servant of God, who never sought the limelight, and who was willing to say, "Here I am, God. Use me."

God favors the humble rather than the proud. God's greatest work in our lives may be difficult and challenging, and we may never receive recognition or the praise of others, but we are called to serve anyway, seeking nothing more than God's satisfaction and glory.

Reflection
Joseph's Dreams

It is not by accident that Matthew tells us that, while Gabriel spoke directly to Mary, Joseph's message came in a dream. We can see a connection between this Joseph and the patriarch Joseph, whose story fills nearly thirteen chapters of Genesis. God spoke to that Joseph in dreams (hence the title of Andrew Lloyd Webber and Tim Rice's musical, *Joseph and the Amazing Technicolor Dreamcoat*), and in a similar way God spoke to Joseph the carpenter in dreams. Matthew looks for these kind of parallels between the Old Testament and the story of Jesus.

Has God ever spoken to you in a dream? I hardly remember the dreams I have when I sleep. But I frequently have what could be called day dreams. Some might call these visions. In them I sometimes see what could be; what I believe God wants to be. These are ideas that come to me while I'm reading Scripture, or hearing someone else preach, or meeting with my small group, or conversing with others. Often these are dreams that come when seeing places of great need. I carry a little black book with me to write down these dreams when they occur, because I quickly forget them.

I pray over these dreams, meditate upon and then test these dreams to see if they appear to be only my ideas, or if it is possible that God has placed these dreams in my heart. I look to see if they line up with Scripture and our church's purpose; if they are personal, I consider how they line up with my personal mission. I share these dreams with my wife and ask for her thoughts. I share them with the lead staff and lay leaders of the church and with my closest friends. All this is a discernment process that helps me avoid chasing after a whim. Over the years, some of the most meaningful and productive things I've been a part of have started with a dream that I felt was from God.

Your dreams may emerge as you hear other people's dreams. Several years ago Karla, one of our staff at the church, felt compelled to start a worship service for senior adults who had Alzheimer's, dementia, or other forms of memory loss. She announced it to area nursing homes, and they began sending buses of people to the worship service in our chapel.

Karla and her team filled the service with well-known hymns, familiar creeds, the Lord's Prayer, and simple messages that might help people remember who they are. Recently the teachers in our daytime Kindermusik program began bringing the little children to sing for this worship service. The three- and four-year-olds sang, "Jesus loves me, this I know, for the Bible tells me so. Little ones to him belong; they are weak but he is strong." As the children sang the chorus, "Yes, Jesus loves me," voices of people who could not remember their own names joined the children: "Yes, Jesus loves me. Yes, Jesus loves me. The Bible tells me so."

The dream of one woman became the dream of a host of volunteers, and together they did what they felt God was leading them to do. The result was something extraordinary.

God spoke to Joseph in dreams. Joseph's dreams called him to devote the rest of his life to nurturing, mentoring, and protecting Jesus. My dreams from God seldom come at night. They are a sense of calling that wells up inside.

Are you listening for God to speak to you? And if God speaks, are you willing to obey? Listening for God's dreams, and following them, made all the difference in Joseph's life, and it makes all the difference in our lives as well.

Lord, help me to listen for your dreams for my life, and give me the boldness and courage to pursue them. Speak, Lord; your servant is listening. Amen.

From *The Journey: A Season of Reflections.* Abingdon Press, 2011.

Travel Notes

Herodium

When you visit Bethlehem today, you'll see Herodium looming over it. Herodium appears to be a mountain, almost like a volcano. But it's not naturally occurring; the mountain was built by human hands!

In Joseph's day, people would have come from miles around to see this marvel. It was Judea's equivalent of the Great Pyramid of Giza in Egypt, and it was constructed shortly before Joseph was born. King Herod built it as a testament to his own greatness to celebrate a victory in battle.

As you climb to the top of Herodium, you can see what remains of the artificial lake and pools that Herod built, as well as the villas where his friends stayed. You see the 900-seat amphitheater built into the side of the mountain—talk about a home theater! At the very top, the king built a palace for himself 400 feet in the air. By comparison, the Great Pyramid of Giza was only 350 feet.

To reach Herod's Palace today, you walk through tunnels in the side of the mountain, ascend stairs, and finally arrive at the palace. There you find storerooms, hot and cold Roman baths, suites, and a veranda from which you can see the little town of Bethlehem. The view is stunning, as it was in the time of Christ.

Travel Photos

Herodium

Top of Herodium

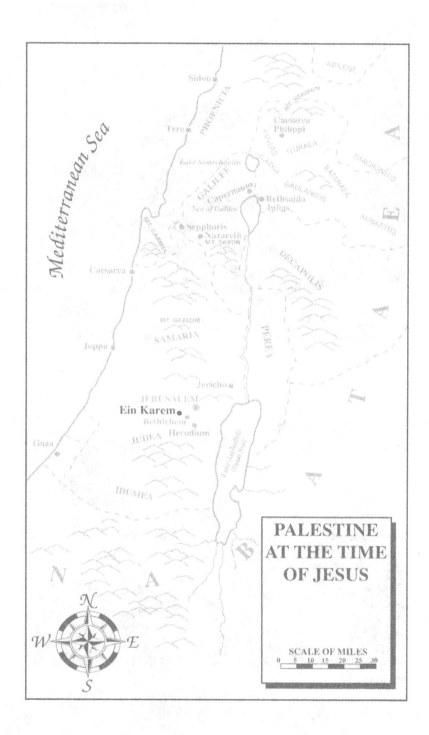

Mediterranean Sea

Sidon

Tyre

PHOENICIA

ABILENE

MT. HERMON

Caesarea
Philippi

PANEAS

ITURAEA

TRACHONITIS

Lake Semechonitis

GAULANITIS

BATANAEA

GALILEE

Capernaum

Sea of Galilee

Bethsaida
Julias

AURANITIS

MT. CARMEL

Sepphoris

Nazareth

MT. TABOR

DECAPOLIS

Caesarea

MT. GERIZIM

SAMARIA

PEREA

Joppa

Jericho

JERUSALEM

Ein Karem

Bethlehem

Herodium

JUDEA

Lake Asphaltitis
(Dead Sea)

Gaza

IDUMEA

N A B A T

**PALESTINE
AT THE TIME
OF JESUS**

SCALE OF MILES

0   5   10 15 20 25 30

N

W   E

S

3. Mary's Visit to Elizabeth

In those days Mary set out and went with haste to a Judean town in the hill country, where she entered the house of Zechariah and greeted Elizabeth. When Elizabeth heard Mary's greeting, the child leaped in her womb. And Elizabeth was filled with the Holy Spirit and exclaimed with a loud cry, "Blessed are you among women, and blessed is the fruit of your womb. And why has this happened to me, that the mother of my Lord comes to me? For as soon as I heard the sound of your greeting, the child in my womb leaped for joy. And blessed is she who believed that there would be a fulfillment of what was spoken to her by the Lord."

(Luke 1:39-45)

Counsel and Comfort

HAVING CONSIDERED JOSEPH'S STORY, let's return to Mary's story in Luke's Gospel. After Mary received word that she was going to give birth to a child—to the long-awaited Messiah—she was likely confused and terrified. Whom could she talk to about what she had heard?

Mary may have recalled that Gabriel, before leaving, had said that Mary's cousin Elizabeth was expecting a child, which was itself a miracle given that Elizabeth was thought to be beyond childbearing years. It seems clear in Luke's Gospel that Mary did not need any further explanation concerning the identity of Elizabeth. Mary must not only have known Elizabeth but felt a genuine closeness to her. Elizabeth may have been an older cousin or even an aunt or great aunt to Mary. Whatever their relationship, it seems clear that Mary and Elizabeth had had significant interaction prior to the Annunciation, for as soon as Mary learned she was pregnant, she "went with haste" to visit Elizabeth.

It is likely that before Mary told her own parents about her pregnancy, she went to find Elizabeth in the hope that Elizabeth would both believe her and help her. Mary knew that if there was one person who would understand, it would be Elizabeth. A second reason for Mary's visit to Elizabeth may have been the proximity of Elizabeth's home and the home of Mary's fiancé, Joseph.

Tradition places the home of Elizabeth and her husband Zechariah in Ein Karem, a village on a hill just a few miles (less than an hour's walk) from the Temple Mount in Jerusalem. Ein Karem is mentioned in Jeremiah 6:1 and Nehemiah 3:14 as "Beth-haccherem." Today, the town is visited by hundreds of thousands of pilgrims each year who go to worship and pray at the churches that mark both Mary's visit to Elizabeth and the place where John the Baptist was born. (Elizabeth and Zechariah were John's parents.) There is also a spring located in this town, known as Mary's Spring.

Ein Karem was eighty miles from Mary's home in Nazareth. This journey by foot would have taken perhaps nine days. Mary would not have traveled alone but would have made the journey with folks who were on their way to Jerusalem. It is likely that Mary explained to her parents that she had learned of Elizabeth's pregnancy and volunteered to go and help her during the pregnancy. How else would she explain to her parents that she wanted to travel so far from home to see Elizabeth? Further, Mary stayed with Elizabeth until the end of Elizabeth's pregnancy, which might indicate that Mary had come to help Elizabeth until the baby was born.

The fact that Mary was willing to travel nine days across three mountain ranges to see Elizabeth speaks volumes about how she was feeling. She longed for someone who might believe her and who could help her make sense of what was happening.

The Elder Elizabeth

Mary was seeking out an older woman, a maternal figure who was not her mother. Elizabeth seems indeed to be the perfect person for Mary to visit. She was married to an older priest named Zechariah, and together they were the New Testament's Abraham and Sarah. Luke tells us that after years of hoping to have children, Elizabeth and Zechariah had resigned themselves to the fact that children were not going to be a part of their lives. Many couples who have been unable to have children of their own treat their nieces and nephews as if they were their own. Perhaps this is why Mary felt drawn to Elizabeth; maybe Elizabeth had been like a mother to Mary in days past.

Before considering Mary's visit, let's take a closer look at Elizabeth's pregnancy. The child born to Elizabeth and Zechariah was the person we know as John the Baptist, born six months before Jesus. John played an important role in preparing the way for Jesus' ministry.

The story of the announcement to Zechariah that he and Elizabeth were to have a child is recorded in Luke 1:5-25. That announcement, like the announcement that came to Mary, came from a heavenly messenger. It occurred while Zechariah was serving as priest in the Temple one day.

It was a special event in the life of a priest to serve in the Temple and offer incense to God. One day Zechariah was chosen for this task. As he was in the Holy Place in the Temple offering sacrifice, he saw a messenger of God standing by him. He was terrified! "Zechariah," the messenger said, "God has heard your prayers. Elizabeth is going to have a child."

I imagine Zechariah saying, "It's a little late for that, you know. I'm an old man, and Elizabeth is too old to have children."

The messenger said, "Because you didn't believe me, you will be unable to speak throughout Elizabeth's pregnancy. But you will see what I have said come to pass; your wife will conceive and bear a son. You will call him John, and he will go before the Messiah to announce his coming." Zechariah emerged from the Temple literally speechless. Before long Elizabeth discovered she was pregnant.

If Elizabeth and Zechariah were like many of the couples I know who have struggled with infertility, it is likely that they had conceived and miscarried on several occasions. The chances of a miscarriage in a pregnancy at their advanced ages was high. This may explain why Elizabeth went into seclusion for the first five months of her pregnancy. Unwilling to subject herself to the pain of another public miscarriage, she decided to wait to celebrate her pregnancy until she had passed the second trimester.

(See Luke 1:24.) It seems to have been Mary's visit that drew Elizabeth out of her seclusion. Mary needed Elizabeth, but perhaps Elizabeth also needed Mary.

Today, if you were to visit the town of Ein Karem, you would find two important churches built there commemorating the events in Luke's Gospel. The Church of the Visitation marks the traditional site of Mary's visit to Elizabeth, where the events described in this chapter are said to have taken place. The other church, the Church of St. John the Baptist, is built atop a grotto that is said to be the place where John was born.

Let's return to Luke's story of Mary's visit to Elizabeth.

Mary Arrives at Elizabeth's Home

After nine days of difficult travel, Mary finally reached Elizabeth's home and announced herself: "Elizabeth, it's me, Mary!" Luke tells us, "When Elizabeth heard Mary's greeting, the child leaped in her womb. And Elizabeth was filled with the Holy Spirit and exclaimed with a loud cry, 'Blessed are you among women, and blessed is the fruit of your womb'" (1:41-42). Elizabeth's words are familiar to Roman Catholics, who recognize in them a portion of the "Hail Mary." (An important side note: Luke records that Elizabeth was "filled with the Holy Spirit." In the Old Testament, prophets and on rare occasions kings were said to be filled with God's Spirit. Here Elizabeth joins their ranks, speaking prophetic words over Mary.)

"And why has this happened to me," Elizabeth continued, "that the mother of my Lord comes to me? For as soon as I heard the sound of your greeting, the child in my womb leaped for joy. And blessed is she who believed that there would be a fulfillment of what was spoken to her by the Lord" (1:43-45).

Mary was, at the most, just a few weeks pregnant, yet already the child forming in her womb had an identity known to

Elizabeth. Elizabeth recognized that the child developing in Mary's womb was none other than "my Lord." Elizabeth was six months pregnant, and the child in her womb responded to the sound of Mary's voice—and by implication to the child in Mary's womb—by kicking. Here, *in utero*, John the Baptist bore witness to the identity of Jesus as the long-awaited Messiah.

It is interesting to note that the first person in all the Gospels to call Jesus "Lord" was Elizabeth, and she proclaimed it even before Jesus was born. This passage sets the stage for the rest of Luke's Gospel, which is the story of the birth, life, teachings, ministry, death, and resurrection of the Lord. Luke's traveling companion, the apostle Paul, notes the importance of the confession that "Jesus is Lord" in his letter to the Romans: "If you confess with your lips that Jesus is Lord and believe in your heart that God raised him from the dead, you will be saved" (Romans 10:9).

Imagine Mary's feelings as she heard Elizabeth's words. It had been at least ten days since Gabriel had appeared to Mary with his confusing announcement. She had spent the last nine days traveling with her secret, uncertain, afraid, and wondering how any of this could be true. But then, before she could even tell Elizabeth what had happened, Elizabeth showed that she knew Mary's secret, and Elizabeth was filled with joy on Mary's behalf. Elizabeth went on to say, in essence, "Listen, child. You don't have to be afraid. You've been blessed. Blessed! Don't you see it? You've been chosen to be the mother of the Messiah. Such good things will come of this! You are so blessed! And the child within your womb is blessed as well!" Twice in Luke 1:42-45 Elizabeth told Mary she was blessed, and once in these same verses she described the child as blessed. (We'll come back to this idea of blessedness in a moment.)

At last, with the prophetic words of Elizabeth, Mary's fear gave way to joy. She opened her mouth and began to praise God. Up to this point we have not heard joy from Mary, only submission to God's will. But now she felt joy that she was going to have a child and, more than that, that her child would be the Messiah. She broke into song: "My soul magnifies the Lord! My spirit rejoices in God my Savior!" (See Luke 1:46-47.)

Mary needed someone who could help her gain perspective on what she was facing; someone who would listen to and believe in her; someone who would encourage her. She found all that and more in her kinswoman Elizabeth.

"The Paradox of Blessedness"

In the short passage from Luke (1:42-45), Elizabeth used the word *blessed* three times to describe Mary and the child she would have: "You are blessed among all women and your child is blessed. Mary, don't you see it? You are really blessed!"

Elizabeth's insistence on driving home that point helped Mary see what William Barclay called "the paradox of blessedness." Sometimes we think God's blessing involves gaining money, power, and prestige. Blessedness is often associated with a life of comfort and ease. When we describe our blessings, they often include our homes, our jobs, our health and wealth. But Mary's blessedness wasn't material. It wasn't born of security or physical well-being. Mary's blessedness came from being a part of God's plan—to be used by God for God's kingdom. Her blessedness was in the fact that she was chosen by God to bear the Messiah.

This blessedness was not to be confused with ease or comfort or a well-being that came from possessions. To the contrary, Mary would face the whispers of those who would know she conceived out of wedlock. She still faced the task of telling Joseph she was with child. She would face the difficulties that came from being the mother of Jesus—fleeing to Egypt when

Herod sought to kill the child, watching as others sought to destroy him when he began his ministry, and finally standing by as he was crucified. This was what blessedness looked like for Mary.

"The piercing truth," says Barclay in a wonderful line from his commentary on Luke, "is that God does not choose a person for ease and comfort and selfish joy but for a task that will take all that head and heart and hand can bring to it."[1]

Abraham is a perfect example. God told him, "I want you to leave behind everything you've known in the Mesopotamian River Valley and go to a land you've never seen before. You're blessed, by the way! Now, go and be a blessing to all the nations of the earth." (See Genesis 12:1-3.)

Look at the people Jesus called blessed. In Luke he said, "Blessed are the poor." (Luke's Gospel does not use the phrase "the poor in spirit" as Matthew's Gospel does; it simply says "the poor.") Jesus said, "Blessed are those who are hungry now. Blessed are those who weep now. Blessed are you when people revile you and say bad things about you and hurt you. Blessed are you, because great is your reward in the kingdom of heaven." (See Luke 6:20-22.)

Jesus was saying, "You are blessed and you can't yet see it. God is going to use your apparent misfortune for something good." He was saying, "God will be with you."

So our task, when we are facing adversity, is to pray, "God, I trust that somehow you can take this and bring good out of it. I trust that you are walking with me." What Jesus seemed to be saying in the Beatitudes was that we, like Mary, are already blessed as we walk through adversity, for God has already promised to walk with us and to use our adversity for his purposes and for our sanctification.

When you pray, "Bless me, Lord" (and likewise when you say to someone else, "May God bless you"), be careful what you pray for. It may be that the blessings of God that you pray for will come with challenges and adversity. Again, God's blessings are not about ease and comfort, but rather about the joy of being a part of God's work, being used by God for God's purposes, and being accompanied by God's presence, particularly in the face of adversity. That is the paradox of blessedness, and it is what we see when the young, pregnant, and unmarried Mary was told by Elizabeth that she was blessed.

Who Is Your Mary? Who Is Your Elizabeth?

There is still more to glean from Mary's visit to Elizabeth. Elizabeth was an older mentor and guide for Mary. She was a source of encouragement, wisdom, and perspective. All of us need an Elizabeth in our lives, an older person who understands, who can guide and encourage and affirm us. Similarly, we all need to be an Elizabeth for a younger person; part of God's purpose for our lives is that we seek to mentor and encourage younger people.

Who is your Elizabeth, the older person who serves as a mentor for you? Who is your Mary, that younger person you're encouraging and investing in?

One of my Elizabeths was a man named Bob Robertson. Bob was my senior pastor when I was in seminary. I served as the youth pastor of the church he led. He encouraged me and believed in me. He mentored me, challenged me, and taught me. When I graduated from seminary, he made phone calls to several bishops encouraging them to consider finding a place to use me in their regions. When I was sent by my bishop to start a new church, Bob called and said, "When things go well, you will find it is hard to celebrate with other pastors—we pastors can be a little insecure when it comes to another's success—so when something really great happens, call me. I'll be your biggest cheerleader. And if something happens and it doesn't go so well, I want you to call me then too. I'm going to listen and care for you, and I'll always be in your corner."

He would call me regularly and say, "Hey! What's going on now? What's happening in the church?" I remember the first time we had three hundred people in worship at the Church of the Resurrection, maybe two or three years into the new church start. I called and said, "Bob, you won't believe it! We had three hundred people today!" I couldn't think of any other person who would understand the way he would. He said, "Wow! That's awesome, Adam! I'm so proud of you."

When things weren't going so well I could call and he'd say, "Hey, it's going to be okay. God's got his hand on you, and you're going to make it through this. You'll come out the other side." He had lived long enough to have a broader perspective on things than I sometimes had.

As our relationship deepened and he grew older, occasionally Bob would call me to talk about things that were going on in his life. He called me when he was assigned to a very large church, and I celebrated with him. But he also called me when things did not go so well in the church. Although he was thirty-five years my senior, I had the chance to say, "Bob, you are a great pastor and you have so many gifts. You changed my life and I owe so much of who I am to you. It's going to be okay. Just keep pressing on."

Bob died several years ago, and I miss him dearly. He was my Elizabeth—a mentor, companion, confidant, and friend. We all need people like this in our lives, and we all need to be this kind of person for others.

When I think of the power of being someone's Elizabeth, I think of a couple in our congregation. They have great musical gifts, and they sang for many years. But when their daughter died in 2004, the music stopped for them. Today the husband writes, "We came to the Church of the Resurrection (several years ago), and the pastors asked us if we could coach other parents who had lost their children. We began to mentor them and try to help them through the difficult journey they were taking. And a funny thing happened. As we helped others, we began to find joy again. And for the first time in six years, we're singing once more." Their healing took place when they began to mentor and care for others.

I think too of Marty Mather, one of the pillars at the church I serve. She's in her early eighties, and over the course of her lifetime she has served as a mentor for hundreds, perhaps thousands, of young people. Younger women and men are drawn to Marty for her wisdom, her encouragement, and her knowledge of God and the Scriptures. As I was reflecting on Elizabeth's story I asked Marty about her own role as a mentor for younger people and she noted, "I simply listen to these young men and women and encourage them." She went on to say, "If they ask for advice, I give it sparingly. Mostly, we just share our lives. And I have never given anything that I did not receive back fourfold. I am working with a young woman now who looks at me like a grandmother, but I so cherish the friendship. The parts of her life she shares with me bring back so many of the events of my life. I get far more than I give."

That's how mentoring works. It blesses the one who is being mentored, but it also blesses the one who is mentoring. And mentoring is not telling younger adults how to do things; that's just being obnoxious. Mentoring is listening, encouraging, and, when asked, offering perspective and ideas. And that is part of what we see in Mary's visit to Elizabeth.

> **That's how mentoring works. It blesses the one who is being mentored, but it also blesses the one who is mentoring.**

I am constantly incorporating the lessons I learn from people such as Marty into my own life. But I also feel a strong compulsion to devote an increasing amount of my time to mentoring younger people. For the last few years I've been building time into my schedule to meet with, and mentor, younger clergy.

At the church I serve we're seeking to incorporate this idea of mentoring into everything we do. A couple of years ago we decided that a third of the members of every committee and team would be over age fifty-five, another third would be thirty-five to fifty-five, and another third would be under thirty-five. We've found that those over fifty-five pass along wisdom and experience to those who are younger, and that the younger members provide new ideas and fresh perspectives to the older members in a kind of reverse mentoring that helps the group stay fresh. We believe this mixture of age groups makes our church stronger. We use the same model of mentoring when it comes to confirmation, Sunday school, choir programs, and staff relationships. I meet with our younger clergy to mentor them, even as I seek their insights and perspectives. Everyone is enriched by the process. We all need an Elizabeth, and we all are called to encourage a Mary.

The Magnificat

As I briefly mentioned earlier, the joy that Mary and Elizabeth shared in that wonderful visitation is commemorated in a church built in Ein Karem at the site believed to be the home of Elizabeth. The Church of the Visitation is built atop an ancient cistern where some traditions say the two women would have drawn water together. Outside, a bronze sculpture shows Mary and Elizabeth greeting one another; and just beyond is a wall with Mary's song, her *Magnificat*, in dozens of different languages.

As I stood watching busloads of visitors, I was struck by the number of women who came to this holy site. I watched as African women embraced each other and as European and Latina women came holding hands or laughing together, often stopping to have their pictures taken near the statue of Mary and Elizabeth.

I was caught in the role of photographer as women began coming and handing me their cameras, asking if I would take their pictures standing next to Mary and Elizabeth. There was such a sense of joy in their hearts as they remembered the story and the important relationship Mary and Elizabeth shared. They immediately seemed to relate this story to their own friendships with one another.

After Elizabeth's words to Mary, Mary broke out in a psalm of praise to God. We call her song the *Magnificat* from the Latin word for "magnify" or praise, based on the way Mary began her psalm: "My soul magnifies the Lord." Mary's song was drawn from a psalm that she likely learned growing up—found in 1 Samuel 2 on the lips of Hannah, the mother of the great prophet Samuel. Hannah, like Elizabeth, had been unable to have children. When God blessed her with a child, she composed a psalm that began, "My heart exults in the LORD; my strength is exalted in my God."

Let's pause for a moment to read carefully Mary's song of praise. In it we see something important about the character of God.

Mary said,

> "My soul magnifies the Lord,
>   and my spirit rejoices in God my Savior,
> for he has looked with favor on the lowliness of his servant.
>   Surely, from now on all generations will call me blessed;
> for the Mighty One has done great things for me,
>   and holy is his name.
> His mercy is for those who fear him
>   from generation to generation.

He has shown strength with his arm;
  he has scattered the proud in the thoughts of their hearts.
He has brought down the powerful from their thrones,
  and lifted up the lowly;
he has filled the hungry with good things,
  and sent the rich away empty.
He has helped his servant Israel,
  in remembrance of his mercy,
according to the promise he made to our ancestors,
  to Abraham and to his descendants forever." (Luke 1:46-55)

The theme of this hymn is one we've seen in Mary's story and also in Joseph's. Mary was from a town so small that it didn't merit a dot on a map. Joseph was a carpenter, someone whose entire net worth could fit into a toolbox. They were working-class people who lived in obscurity, from families that scraped to get by. And yet these were the people God chose to be the earthly parents of the Messiah. What does that tell us about the character of God? The answer burst forth from Mary's heart. She was simply putting voice to what she had felt and experienced—that God favors and is merciful toward the humble and those who fear him. But he scatters the proud and pulls down the mighty from their thrones.

This is a reversal of fortunes found often in the Gospels, where those who lift themselves up are brought down and those who humble themselves are lifted up. We see it throughout Jesus' teachings, when he says, "The first shall be last and the last shall be first"; "If you really want to be great you will become the servant of others"; "If you're invited to a wedding banquet, take the lowest seat. Then maybe the master will call you and ask you to sit at the head table. But if you place yourself at the head table, the master may tell you to go sit at the lowest table"; and " 'Humble yourself in the sight of the Lord,' the Scripture says, 'and he will lift you up in due time.' " (See Matthew 20:16, 26; Luke 14:8-11; James 4:10.)

In Mary's *Magnificat* we find a picture of a God who has a heart for the underdog and is concerned about people who have been made to feel like nobodies. Those are the ones he lifts up. That is the character of the God proclaimed in the Scriptures. That is the character of his Son.

One line in Mary's song troubles me as someone serving as senior pastor of a predominantly middle- and upper-middle-income congregation. She sings, "He has filled the hungry with good things, and sent the rich away empty." I love the first part of the line; that's exactly what I'm counting on God to do—care for the hungry. But it's the second half that really troubles me, in which God sends the rich away empty. Let's face it: Relative to the rest of the world, most of you reading this book are "the rich." I am among them. I don't want to be sent away empty.

So, what does Mary's song mean for "the rich"? I see her words as an invitation. It is an invitation for us to humble ourselves before God and to be used by God to fulfill the first words of that line—to help the poor walk away full. I am called to share my resources and to pass along the blessings I've received. In seeking to bless and encourage and lift up other people, they are sent away full and I discover what it means to be blessed.

Jesus tells a parable of the Last Judgment, in which he warns that on the last day the nations will stand before him to be judged. He will say to those who did nothing to help others, "I was hungry and thirsty, naked and sick, I was in prison and a stranger, and you turned your back on me. Therefore, I never knew you." He sends those people away empty. But then he says to another group, "I was hungry and thirsty and naked and sick, a stranger and in prison, and you welcomed me and loved me and cared for me. Enter into your rest. Well done, my servants." (See Matthew 25:31-46.)

The *Magnificat* is a powerful reminder of an important dimension of God's character and of God's calling on the lives of his people. God cares for those who have been made to feel small by others and those who have nothing. God uses people to send the hungry away full. And God calls those who, in the eyes of the world, have been successful, to humble ourselves, to lift others up, and to bless and help those in need.

How Much?

As each Christmas approaches and we do our Christmas shopping, most of us at one time or another ask ourselves, What do we buy for people who have everything, who could go out and buy whatever they want? We ask, How much is enough for our kids? How much is too much? Do we have an equal number of gifts for our children, and did we spend the same amount on each?

For many of us the Christmas season is focused on purchasing gifts for people who don't need anything. Then on Christmas morning, the day meant to celebrate the birth of Jesus, we celebrate with an orgy of gift giving and opening that leaves our children numb. Many years as our children were growing up, my wife, LaVon, and I would get to the end of Christmas Day with a kind of sick feeling that we had once again gone overboard with gifts and failed to teach our children what Christmas really means. We would pledge ourselves to "do better next year"; but the next year would roll around and once more we'd feel that we needed to buy, buy, buy in order for our children to know that they were loved.

Over the years, we sought to change this yearly ritual in our lives and in the church I serve. We began to be more intentional about devoting a portion of what we spend on our family at Christmas to share with people in need. We involved our children in the process of picking out gifts for others and in determining where our Christmas giving would go. We began planning to give to those in need an amount equal to or greater than what we would spend on our family and friends for Christmas.

Our church voted a few years ago to give away our entire Christmas Eve candlelight service offering to projects benefiting children in poverty. We challenge worshipers to discover the true spirit of Christmas and to give generously to support two projects, one of which is generally in a developing nation and the other in the inner city of Kansas City.

The year I wrote this book, we gave half of the offering to support building schools, churches, wells, and community gardens among those living in extreme poverty in the African nation of Malawi. At the Christmas Eve service we showed photos and video we'd taken of these children on a recent trip to Malawi, so that worshipers could see the children their offerings would be benefiting. The second half of our Christmas Eve offering was devoted to projects in several inner-city schools where most of the children live below the poverty line. We built playgrounds and nursing stations; provided books, coats, and gloves; and supplied tutors to help children who were struggling in school.

Each year, we invite our people not only to give their money but their time by going with us to Malawi, or by serving as tutors or helping in construction and renovation of school buildings in Kansas City. Our congregation has found this tradition to be invigorating. Our visitors at Christmas Eve feel drawn to this mission and, through it, learn something about our congregation's heart. As a result, our offerings on Christmas Eve have more than doubled.

A couple of years ago, a man came to me after Christmas Eve and said, "I'm an atheist. I came tonight because my friends invited me. I was moved by the service—the music, the message, the candle lighting were all very inspiring. But what I found most amazing was that you gave away your entire offering to children in poverty. I'll be back." I hear stories like this each year.[2]

God has a special concern for the poor, the humble, and those whom others overlook. If we are truly to celebrate Christmas and honor the generous spirit of Mary's *Magnificat,* we must look at ways we can be used by God to "send the hungry away full."

Reflection
How Mary Found Her Joy

For nine or ten days Mary had carried in her heart the most astounding secret: She was pregnant, and the child was to be the long-awaited messianic king, Israel's deliverer. Yet she had been afraid to share the news, for if the wrong person heard, Herod could have had her killed; or, if her loved ones didn't believe her, the religious leaders might have condemned her and had her put to death. Perhaps she herself was afraid to trust that it was true.

But when Elizabeth prophesied over Mary and announced that she was blessed, Mary finally was able to trust that God really was at work. She believed that, despite the inherent danger in carrying the Messiah; despite the reality that her hopes and dreams had been turned upside down; and despite the fact that she didn't fully understand, God would work through her and her child. In her acceptance of this amazing truth, Mary finally shouted out her song of joy. Can you hear the tone of her song in its opening words? "My soul magnifies the Lord! My spirit rejoices in God my Savior!"

Joy, unlike happiness, can come to us independent of our circumstances. It comes not from changing our circumstances but from viewing them through the eyes of faith. The apostles, after being beaten by the Council, rejoiced because they were counted worthy to suffer for the name of Jesus. Paul penned his well-known "epistle of joy"—the Letter to the Philippians—even as he sat in a Roman prison awaiting news as to whether he would be executed for his faith. In the letter he wrote, "Rejoice in the Lord always!" Paul wrote to the Christians at Thessalonica, who themselves had been persecuted for their faith, "Rejoice always," and then told them how this was possible when he continued, "Pray without ceasing" and "give thanks in all circumstances."

Last year I was in Malawi, Africa, visiting rural villages to explore partnerships with local congregations to build wells, schools, and churches. In one of the villages, the people, who earn about fifty-five cents per person per day, took us to the stream of green, brackish water that they used for drinking, cooking, and cleaning. They asked us to consider helping them build a well so their children might not get sick from the water anymore.

After we had toured their village, they invited us to their church. We stepped inside the mud-brick building. It was just a large room with open holes where windows might go, and daylight shining through gaps in the thatched roof. And then they began to worship. They sang songs of utter joy despite their circumstances. They sang songs of joy because they trusted God, and they believed that God had brought us to Malawi to help them have safe drinking water (something we ourselves believed). Would that Christians in the United States sang with such exuberance and joy!

Mary, despite dangers, fears, risks, and upended dreams, "magnified the Lord and rejoiced in God." She did this with the help of Elizabeth and with her own willingness to trust that God was working in and through her to accomplish his purposes.

Joy is a choice we make when we look at our present circumstances through the eyes of faith, trusting that God is at work and that he will never leave us nor abandon us. And it is often found with the help of another who reassures us that God is with us.

Lord, I thank you, even now, for your blessings in my life. Help me to see past my circumstances, to what you will do with and through them. Help me to trust you. Use my adversity for your glory. Amen.

From *The Journey: A Season of Reflections.* Abingdon Press, 2011.

Travel Notes

Ein Karem

Tradition places the home of Elizabeth and her husband Zechariah in Ein Karem, a village on a hill just a few miles (less than an hour's walk) from the Temple Mount in Jerusalem. Today the town is visited by hundreds of thousands of pilgrims who go to worship and pray at two important churches that commemorate events described in the Gospel of Luke. There is also a spring located in this town, known as Mary's Spring.

The Church of St. John the Baptist is built over a grotto that is said to be the place where John was born. (Elizabeth and Zechariah were John's parents.) And the Church of the Visitation marks the traditional site of Mary's visit to Elizabeth.

The Church of the Visitation is built atop an ancient cistern where some say Mary and Elizabeth would have drawn water together. Outside, a bronze sculpture shows the two women greeting one another, and just beyond is a wall with Mary's song, her *Magnificat*, in dozens of different languages.

The *Magnificat* is a powerful reminder of God's character and of God's calling on the lives of his people.

Travel Photos

Ein Karem

Church of St. John the Baptist, Ein Karem

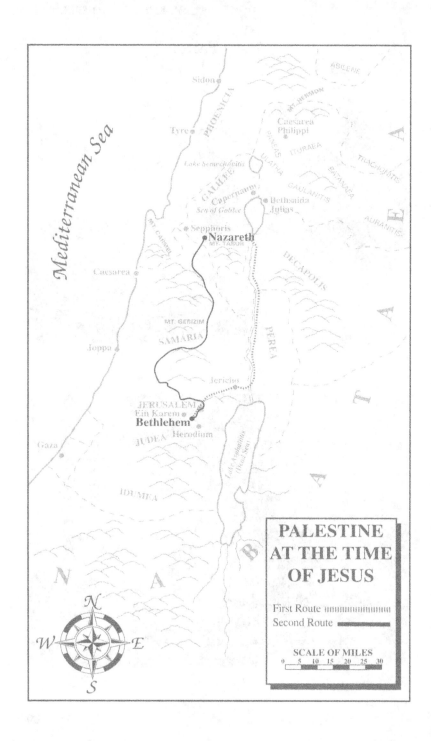

PALESTINE
AT THE TIME
OF JESUS

First Route ⅏⅏⅏⅏⅏⅏⅏⅏⅏
Second Route ▬▬▬

SCALE OF MILES
0   5   10   15   20   25   30

4. From Nazareth to Bethlehem

In those days a decree went out from Emperor Augustus that all the world should be registered. This was the first registration and was taken while Quirinius was governor of Syria. All went to their own towns to be registered. Joseph also went from the town of Nazareth in Galilee to Judea, to the city of David called Bethlehem, because he was descended from the house and family of David. He went to be registered with Mary, to whom he was engaged and who was expecting a child. While they were there, the time came for her to deliver her child. And she gave birth to her first-born son and wrapped him in bands of cloth, and laid him in a manger, because there was no place for them in the inn.

(Luke 2:1-7)

A Hastily Planned Wedding

As WE HAVE SEEN, it was probably during Mary's stay with Elizabeth in Ein Karem that Joseph visited from nearby Bethlehem and learned that Mary was pregnant. We can imagine how he felt, and we are reminded that God is often most profoundly at work in those times when we're confused, broken, or wounded.

When Joseph returned to Bethlehem, he had a dream in which God's messenger confirmed Mary's story and called Joseph to accept Mary and, by implication, to raise Jesus as his own son. Joseph awoke from the dream, went back to Ein Karem, and agreed to take Mary as his wife.

Shortly after Joseph told Mary his dream, he likely would have announced to his family that he and Mary were expediting the wedding and thus would be traveling to Nazareth soon. Did Joseph explain to his parents that Mary was pregnant? We don't know, but even if he had, would they have believed him? Would you believe your son or daughter if they explained that a pregnancy came mysteriously when an angel announced it? The answer is probably no. (This answer may give us a bit more patience with people who doubt the doctrine of the virgin birth. After all, even the righteous Joseph did not believe until he'd had his dream.)

Joseph and Mary made the nine-day journey back to Nazareth, where their wedding was hastily planned and the two were soon married. It is likely that guests, neighbors, and the people of Nazareth whispered about this wedding and suspected that Mary was pregnant. Did Mary and Joseph try to explain the circumstances of Mary's pregnancy? Perhaps. If they did, would the townspeople have believed them?

It was not unheard of in those days for an engaged couple to be found pregnant before the wedding day. The fact that they were formally engaged meant that, for legal purposes, they were already married. Thus a pregnancy, after the formal engagement, was less scandalous than a pregnancy where there was no formal engagement as yet.

We can surmise that Mary may have been about five months pregnant on the day she was married. (She traveled nine days to Elizabeth's home, spent three months there, journeyed nine days back, and then probably spent several weeks to pull together the wedding ceremony.) Several dozen of the more than three hundred weddings I've officiated over in the last twenty years were expedited by the pending birth of a child. While the circumstances that led to Mary's pregnancy were different from these, I began to see that these young women might feel a special connection with Mary, sharing with her this reversal of the traditional order of things.

After the Wedding

In the first century, a couple who wed would typically move in with the husband's parents in a room he would add to their home, until he could afford to acquire land and build a home for his wife and family. We would have expected Joseph and Mary to take up residence in Bethlehem after the formal ceremony. But we know from Luke's Gospel that they remained in Nazareth after the wedding, and it seems reasonable to suppose that they did so because Mary was five months pregnant. The journey to Bethlehem, after all, would have taken about ten days and placed a great strain on her at this advanced stage of the pregnancy. Perhaps more importantly, remaining in Nazareth would have allowed Mary's mother to be nearby and would have given Mary an opportunity to use a midwife she knew.

Luke's Gospel indicates that Mary and Joseph settled into life in Nazareth during the final trimester of Mary's pregnancy. Joseph may have been working in Sepphoris as a carpenter while

Mary stayed in Nazareth to prepare for the day her child would be born.

Mary's Parents

Nothing is said about Mary's parents in the New Testament. The Gospels only mention Mary's relative, Elizabeth, and perhaps Mary's sister, who is thought, by joining John 19:25 with Mark 15:40, to be called Salome. Where there is a vacuum of information in the Gospels, Christians in the second and third centuries began to fill in the details. Some of these details may have been accurate, but many undoubtedly were not.

Among the earliest works seeking to fill in the gaps is the Gospel of James (also referred to as the Proto-Evangelium of James or the Infancy Gospel of James). This book appears to have been written about A.D. 150, and it purports to be written by James, the brother (or half-brother, as the book asserts) of Jesus. Though even the Christians of that time did not accept the book as authentic, it did become extremely popular among the people of the second and third centuries. The text can be read online.

The Gospel of James begins by describing Mary's parents, giving their names as Anna and Joachim, an older couple who, like Abraham and Sarah (and Elizabeth and Zechariah), were unable to have children. God miraculously blessed them with a child, Mary, whom they dedicated to God. When Mary was three years old, they took her to live in the Temple, where she was dedicated to God. There she was looked after by the priests until she was twelve, at which time, since she was becoming a young woman, they decided she could not continue to live there. (Menstruation would make her "unclean" for a week each month. Further, it would have been deemed inappropriate for a young woman to be living among the priests.) Because Mary was holy to God (and hence, by the second-century Christian mind, would never have marital relations), the priests sought to find her an elderly widower to marry. They drew lots, and the elderly Joseph was chosen. According to the Gospel of James, Joseph already had children by a previous wife, which was an early attempt to explain the mention of Jesus' brothers and sisters in the Gospels.

There is more to the story, much of which is clearly fabricated. But it is possible there could be fragments found in this and other second-century works that were rooted in historical fact. While the early church recognized that the Gospel of James was written long after the time of James, and that much in it was pious myth, the names for Mary's parents, Anna and Joachim, stuck. (Another interesting work, the author of which built upon the story in the Gospel of James, is called the History of Joseph the Carpenter, written, it is thought, sometime in the early 400s. It is this work that presents Joseph as 90 when he was chosen to be Mary's husband and 111 when he died.)

Protestant scholars don't put much stock in the value of these books in terms of helping us understand what actually happened with Mary and Joseph, but they do recognize that these documents help us understand how second-, third-, fourth-, and even fifth-century Christians were thinking about Mary and Joseph's story.

The Census

In the ninth month of Mary's pregnancy, Roman soldiers arrived in Nazareth to announce that the emperor had commanded a census and that every Jewish family must return to the husband's hometown to be counted. The census was for the purpose of levying taxes, and thus it is likely that the Romans wished for all families to return to the location of their property. Joseph's property—that is, Joseph's portion of his father's estate and the carpentry business they may have shared—was in Bethlehem. Mary, being the wife of Joseph, was now a part of his family. She was bound to return with Joseph to his hometown of Bethlehem.

In recounting this part of the story, Luke reminds us of several things. First, Palestine—the Holy Land—was at that time an occupied territory of the Roman Empire. The people within its borders were not free. They did what the Romans told them to do. Most were not Roman citizens. They had limited rights. They could be forced to serve Romans, and they certainly were required to pay Roman taxes. By telling us about the Roman census, Luke explains how Jesus came to be born in Bethlehem, not Nazareth. At the same time, Luke helps us see Mary and Joseph as a poor couple who were forced to travel ten days, when she was nine months pregnant, out of fear of what would happen to them if they did not.

What do you think Mary was feeling as Joseph explained that, though she was nine months pregnant, they both would have to make the ten-day journey to Bethlehem? Mary didn't know a midwife in Bethlehem, was physically uncomfortable, and was undoubtedly anxious about having her baby so far from home.

Mary had prayed the *Magnificat* when she was with Elizabeth just after discovering she was pregnant. But what would her prayer have been now? I picture Mary breaking down in tears and shouting, "God, how could you? You came and asked me to bear this child, and I agreed. I said, 'Here I am, the handmaiden of the Lord.' I took on the shame that went with a hurried marriage, enduring the looks and whispers as I walked by the people in the community. And now, I won't be able to have my baby in Nazareth? You had to take that away too? Why is this happening? What did I do that was so wrong? Why, God? Why did you not change the emperor's mind? Why did you not protect me from this? How can you let this happen?"

Have you ever felt this way toward God? Have you ever found yourself so profoundly disappointed that all you could do was cry out in anger to God, or weep, or both? The Gospels don't tell us this is how Mary felt. They tell us nothing. We're left to imagine, to put ourselves in Mary's sandals and to imagine what she felt. What is a young woman, nine months pregnant, a jumble of hormones, going to feel as she hears once more that the one thing she thought she could control—where she would give birth and who would be with her—was now being stripped away by an emperor's edict in Rome?

Yet, as we will see, what appeared to Mary as profoundly disappointing is today one of the most compelling parts of the story of Jesus' birth—that Mary and Joseph were forced to travel to Bethlehem and that Mary would give birth in a stable. And because of this edict, the story unfolded quite differently than it might have otherwise. There is a deeper meaning to these events that Mary can't understand yet. God is taking the decision of a greedy emperor and forcing it to serve God's own saving purposes, which is precisely what God does in our lives as well.

Which Route to Bethlehem?

There were two possible routes Joseph and Mary might have taken to Bethlehem. You can see them both on the map at the beginning of this chapter. (There was a third route, but the two I describe here are most often mentioned by scholars.)

The first route, which is shown as a dotted line on the map, would have taken Mary and Joseph to the east, crossing the Jordan, then south sixty miles, and finally recrossing the Jordan near Jericho and west to Bethlehem. This route would have been followed by Jews wishing to avoid the land of the Samaritans, a people of mixed descent whose faith was largely influenced by Judaism but that had its own distinctive elements. The land of the

Samaritans—Samaria—separated the northern region of Galilee from the southern region of Judea. Many Jews considered the Samaritans unclean, or heretics, or worse. Because of the conflict with Samaritans, some Jews felt it might be dangerous to travel through Samaria; hence, for purity or safety many Jews went out of their way to avoid passing through it. But taking this route around Samaria would have added twenty or thirty miles to Mary and Joseph's journey—perhaps two days.

This first route is assumed by many pastors, teachers, and biblical scholars to be the route that Joseph and Mary would have taken. Some argue that this route along the Jordan would also have been easier to travel because the Jordan River valley is a plain, and there is some truth to this. But having taken both routes, I would point out that each has its challenges.

The second route, and the one I think likely, which is shown as a solid line on the map, was the more direct route. It took them nearly due south from Nazareth through the Jezreel Valley and along the road known as the Way of the Patriarchs. This route was easier through the first half of the journey, though the second half included some hills and mountains, with well-known places to stop for water along the way. This route would have meant two fewer days of travel than the first route described.

While in Bethlehem researching this book, I had coffee with noted archaeologist Avner Goren to discuss this question of the route Mary and Joseph might have taken on their journey. As we talked about the two routes, he too leaned toward the Way of the Patriarchs as the likely route of the Holy Family.

In addition to this being the more direct route, there are several other reasons for thinking that Mary and Joseph traveled through the heart of Samaria to reach Bethlehem. The first-century Jewish historian Josephus is said to have noted that during the Passover, when large numbers of Jews were making their way to Jerusalem, it was not uncommon for Jews to go through Samaria. His mention of this points to the fact that faithful Jews were willing to pass through Samaria when there were large numbers of people traveling, perhaps to avoid the "traffic jams" they might have encountered on the other route resulting from

In following the route through Samaria, the Holy Family would have been retracing sixteen hundred years of biblical history.

the hundreds of caravans trying to make their way south. The census that forced Mary and Joseph to travel would have affected hundreds if not thousands of others in Galilee who would be trying to make their way south.

As I traveled the Way of the Patriarchs myself, I was moved by this thought: In following the route through Samaria, the Holy Family would have been retracing sixteen hundred years of biblical history. It was in this area, in the center of the country, that God appeared to Abraham and promised to give this land to his descendants. Here Jacob saw angels ascending and descending to and from heaven. Mary and Joseph's caravan made camp near springs and wells each night that had been used since the time of the patriarchs, including "Jacob's Well" near the town of Sychar.

They passed the place where Joseph, the son of Jacob, whose story we recall from the Old Testament, was buried after his bones were brought back from Egypt. They came to Shiloh, where Joshua had set up the tent of meeting and the ark of the covenant. They walked where the great early prophets Samuel, Elijah, and Elisha ministered. They followed the path of the Assyrian army when it came to destroy the Northern Kingdom of Israel and where the armies of Babylon marched as they invaded Judea and Jerusalem itself and carried away its people. But they also retraced the steps of the exiles who returned "singing unto Zion" after the Exile was over. God walked with his people through all these journeys.

Thus the journey that I believe Mary and Joseph took to Bethlehem would have been both a recounting, geographically, of what scholars refer to as God's "salvation history" and at the same time, because of the child in Mary's womb, the apex of this history!

There is one last reason I feel it likely that Joseph and Mary traversed this route through the heart of Samaria rather than going around it. To go around Samaria would have meant that Joseph and Mary, like so many Jews of the time, felt that Samaritans were unclean and therefore to be avoided—so much so that, though Mary was nine months pregnant, they would add two days to their trip simply to avoid Samaria. Was this how Mary and Joseph saw the Samaritans?

I was reminded of Jesus' own attitude toward the Samaritans. In John's Gospel, Chapter 4, Jesus passed through Samaria and stopped at a well near the town of Sychar—it was Jacob's Well—and offered a Samaritan woman "living water by which you will never thirst again." (See John 4:10, 14.) This woman had been divorced five times and was now living with a man. She had been emotionally wounded and was searching for something to satisfy her soul. Jesus offered it to her and then called her to go to her people and tell them about him—in essence, to become the first missionary to the Samaritans.

I was also reminded of Jesus' scandalous parable of the good Samaritan, in which he made a Samaritan man the great example of what it means to "love your neighbor as you love yourself," showing the Samaritan to be more righteous than either a Jewish priest or a Levite.

As I thought of Jesus' attitude and actions toward Samaritans, I wondered where he would have learned to see Samaritans with compassion and to recognize that they were children of God. I suspect he first learned these things from his mother and earthly father. Jesus' attitude toward Samaritans, if it was a reflection of his parents' own way of seeing Samaritans, would make it unlikely that Mary and Joseph would have traveled out of their way along the Jordan route to avoid contact with Samaritans.

Here's a question worth pondering as we reflect upon Mary and Joseph's journey through Samaria and upon Jesus' attitude toward Samaritans: Who are our Samaritans? And where is our Samaria? In other words, which groups do we feel an aversion for, and where are the places in our own city, country, or world that we would avoid because we are uncomfortable with "those people"?

In so many ways today's Palestinians are modern-day Samaritans. Much of the West Bank was Samaria in the time of Jesus. The conflict between Jews and Palestinians defines life in the Holy Land today. Like so many first-century Jews, American Christians avoid passing through the West Bank territories or staying in West Bank towns like Bethlehem while visiting the Holy Land. Few of us have taken the time to understand the conflict.

The Journey

In my trip to the Holy Land to research this book, we traveled by car, by van, and on foot as we sought to follow the journey Mary and Joseph would have taken from Nazareth to Bethlehem. Luke does not mention the presence of a donkey, though it seems likely that Joseph would have procured an animal to help Mary make the journey. (The previously mentioned apocryphal Gospel of James does mention a donkey.)

Their journey began with a descent from the hills of Nazareth to the smooth plain of the Jezreel Valley. This would have been the easiest part of the journey and may have taken the first two days. The Jezreel Valley was the location of so many ancient battles that it became synonymous with war and bloodshed. The writer of Revelation saw the final, apocalyptic battle between good and evil—the battle of Armageddon—taking place here. (*Armageddon* means "hill of Megiddo," with Megiddo being a city built upon a hill along the Jezreel Valley—see Revelation 16:16.)

As we passed through this valley, I was reminded that the child in Mary's womb would be called the Prince of Peace; yet it was also this child who John claimed would one day return, riding on a white horse, to wage a righteous war against evil and ultimately to triumph over it (Revelation 19:11-16).

As Mary and Joseph began the slow ascent from the Jezreel Valley, they would have walked past mile after mile of olive trees, planted in groves along the road. The oldest of the trees that still exist today are said to date back to the time of Christ. The olive trees, like the journey itself, bore witness to the child in Mary's womb.

The extra-virgin oil from the olives was used in the anointing of kings; in fact, the word *Messiah* means "Anointed One." (The Greek word *Christ* means the same.) Pouring or smearing sacred oil on a person or an object signified that the individual or object was holy to God and set apart for God's purposes. Kings were typically anointed by the high priest, though David was anointed by Samuel the prophet. Jesus, however, was anointed by a prostitute in Luke 7:36-50 and by Lazarus's sister Mary in John 11:1-2 (and presumably in Mark 14:3). These incidents were important statements about Jesus' concern for sinners and those whom Jewish society considered to be second class; Jesus valued these persons so highly that they were given the privilege of anointing him as king. Oil was also used in healing prayer, and Jesus' own disciples would use olive oil to anoint the sick under his direction.

After several days, the journey to Bethlehem would have become more challenging, following the ancient road that curved back and forth as it ascended and descended the hills and mountains of central Israel. Each day's journey would have ended at a spring or well that could provide for the needs of all the people and animals in the caravan. We stopped at two such places on our journey to retrace Mary and Joseph's steps. The first was an oasis, a spring that is said to have provided water for Abraham and his descendants in the center of the West Bank. The second was Jacob's Well in Sychar, where Jesus met the Samaritan woman. I have always loved this story; but because my previous trips to the Holy Land bypassed the West Bank (except Bethlehem), I had never seen the well before.

The grade of the city of Sychar has risen over the centuries with the destruction and rebuilding of city upon city. Today, the well is beneath a magnificent church built by the Russian Orthodox. Descending a set of steps to the left of the altar, visitors come to a room with an ancient well. There, a bucket is attached to a rope, and when lowered for what must be one hundred feet, it finally takes on water. As I drew water from the well, I imagined Joseph and Mary drinking from this same water source as they rested here for the night. Little did Mary know that, thirty years later, the child in her womb would stand here, offering living water to a Samaritan woman.

Mary and Joseph continued on their journey from Sychar, traveling for the next three days over ever-higher hills. As if to help us imagine the challenge of the journey, our Palestinian driver's van threatened to break down on the highest of these mountains. We had to stop and let the engine cool off before starting up again, which gave us a chance to walk about, taking in the stark hillsides over which Mary and Joseph must have crossed. We had passed from the verdant country in the north to the hot and arid country that typifies the southern part of the

Holy Land. For Mary, this would have been the most difficult and uncomfortable part of the journey. The Holy Family would have been traveling now for seven days. "Soon," Joseph must have assured Mary, "we'll be going down to Bethel, and then on to Jerusalem and Bethlehem. We're going to make it. You'll be fine, Mary."

On the afternoon of the ninth day, or early on the morning of the tenth, Mary and Joseph finally must have seen Jerusalem. I can only imagine how they felt as they saw the Holy City spread out before them. Jerusalem was of course much smaller in the first century. It was a city set upon a hill—actually multiple hills—but the eye was naturally drawn to one hill, Mount Moriah, where the Temple rose high above everything else. Every time I come to Jerusalem, I find that my heart beats faster. I am mysteriously drawn to this place. It represents God's earthly dwelling place—a symbol of God's presence—and the place where so much that is important to my faith took place. Mary and Joseph likely would have felt the same way.

From Jerusalem, it would have been only a few hours' walk to Bethlehem, across several miles of arid desert and some hills. Finally, on perhaps the tenth day of their journey, they would have arrived in Bethlehem.[1]

Room in the Inn?

Joseph and Mary finally reached Bethlehem. Luke tells us only that "while they were there, the time came for her to deliver her child" (2:6). We don't know if she began going into labor upon her arrival in Bethlehem, or if they had been there for several days before this occurred. We typically think of the story in this way: Joseph and Mary arrive in Bethlehem, and Joseph, being a typical guy, has not made reservations in advance at the local inn. The city is brimming with visitors, and hence there is no room in the inn. The innkeeper offers them space in the stable, and it is there that the baby was born.

This is the version of the story that most of us have grown up with, and parts of it certainly are true. Mary did give birth in a stable, and she laid the Christ Child in a feeding trough. However, there is some debate about whether Mary and Joseph could find no room in the inn, and for that matter whether it was an "inn" at all.

In Chapter 2, you rightly may have asked: If Joseph was from Bethlehem, why would he and Mary have needed to stay at an inn? Wouldn't they have stayed with Joseph's family? It's a great question, and the answer changes how we read this story.

The Greek word that is translated in most versions of Luke's Gospel as "inn" is *kataluma*. This word's only other appearance in the Gospels comes when Jesus sends his disciples ahead to find a room they can use for their Last Supper together. That room, as you'll recall, was not a room in an inn, but a guest room in a house. This is the more accurate translation of *kataluma*—it is a guest room.

It may be helpful at this point to see what a simple first-century home looked like. (See the drawing on page 111; it is based on the archaeological remains of a first-century home.) There would be a central room that served as kitchen and living area. Off of that room would be the sleeping quarters, where parents slept. Typically there would be a guest room where children slept, but which they yielded to guests when there was company. This was the *kataluma*. When there were guests, the children slept with the parents or in the main living space. There was also a stable, or a small barn—think of it as a garage—that was either behind the home or, in the case of homes built atop or around caves, beneath the home. The stable protected the animals from predators and thieves at night.

Assuming that Joseph's family was of modest income, they would have had one guest room. The guest room might hold bed mats for six people sleeping side by side. The main living room and kitchen could hold several more. Here's the question: How many of Joseph's extended family were in Bethlehem because of the census? If Joseph had four or five siblings and each of them had family, it is easy to see why there would have been no room in the *kataluma*.

Another argument can be made for why, even if the house was not overcrowded, Joseph's family would have set up a room in the stable in which Mary could give birth. Leviticus 12:1-7 notes that when a woman gives birth to a son, she becomes unclean until her child is circumcised on the eighth day after he is born. It is the discharge of blood and water at childbirth that causes her to be ritually unclean, just as a woman was considered ritually impure or unclean during her monthly period. Leviticus 15:19-23 notes that anyone who touches a woman who has a "flow of blood" will also become ritually unclean until evening. Further, anything she lies on becomes unclean. Anything that touches her becomes unclean. Anyone who touches anything she lies on becomes unclean. You begin to see the problem with Mary's giving birth in the guest room, where everyone else would have planned to sleep. Giving birth in the guest room renders the room and all who touch anything in it unclean.

It seems likely, then, that Joseph's parents would have set up a birthing room in the barn to give Mary and Joseph privacy and to keep everyone and everything in the house from becoming ritually unclean. For a poor family with limited resources and only a single guest room, the stable may have been the best option they could offer.

Understanding this, I still imagine, as Mary sat on the birthing stool, that between contractions she must have been forcing

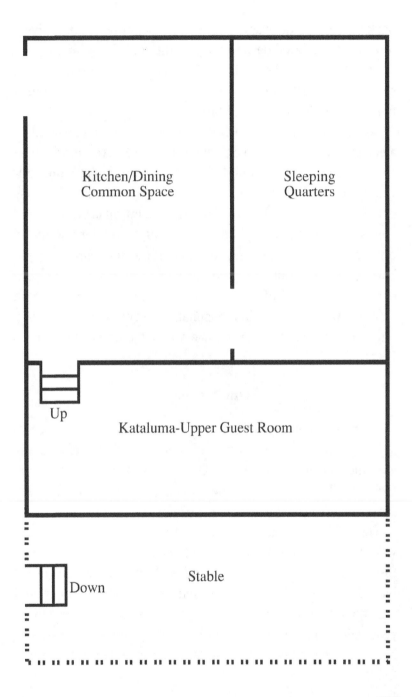

Kitchen/Dining
Common Space

Sleeping
Quarters

Up

Kataluma-Upper Guest Room

Down

Stable

back the tears. This was not how it was supposed to be—giving birth in her in-laws' barn. I imagine the midwife saying to her, "Child, it's going to be all right. Trust me. I've delivered in worse settings. At least you have your privacy. I'm here, and God is here, and you're going to be fine."

Several years ago I preached a series of sermons inspired by a line from Andrew Peterson's song "Labor of Love," in which he sang, "It was not a silent night." This was not a silent night. Our Christmas carols sometimes miss the reality of what Mary was experiencing that night. We sing, "All is calm, all is bright round yon virgin, mother and child. Holy infant, so tender and mild," but it was not like that. It was disappointing and depressing and hard. Life can be that way. And the long-awaited Messiah's birth came in the midst of the messiness and disappointment and pain. He was born, not in a hospital, not even in a guest room, but in a stable, among the animals, with a feeding trough for his first bed.

Our Journeys

In the midst of the hardship that went with Mary and Joseph's journey, amid the deferred dreams and dashed hopes, God was working to redeem the world. God forces every circumstance, including the oppression of the Roman government, to serve his purpose.

This was not a journey Mary wanted to take. It was not the way she imagined it would be. And of course this was not to be the last of Mary's unwanted journeys. A short time after Jesus' birth, Herod would try to kill the child, and she and Joseph would take the infant Jesus and flee to Egypt as refugees. Thirty-three years later, there would be another journey she would take with her son, this time down the *Via Dolorosa* as she followed him to Calvary.

We will each take unwanted journeys in life. I think of those I know who have been laid off work; those who are battling cancer; a family whose child has struggled with drug addiction; people I see each week whose spouses have left; parents who have lost children. You know plenty of others, I'm sure. Life will have its moments of disappointment, its times of overwhelming sorrow and intense pain. But the good news of Scripture is that God not only walks with us on these journeys; God redeems them and brings good from them. The Bible is filled with such stories.

Jacob's son Joseph was sold as a slave by his brothers, then wound up in Egypt, falsely accused and thrown into prison. But that was not the end of Joseph's story.

David fled into the wilderness when King Saul tried to kill him. He stayed among the Philistines for a couple of years, writing psalms that asked God, "Why do you allow my enemies to prosper? When are you going to save me?" He did not want to take this journey. But that was not the end of David's story.

Shadrach, Meshach, and Abednego were told to bow down and worship the Babylonian king's image; if they refused they would be thrown into the fiery furnace. Surely they did not wish to take this journey to the fiery furnace. But that was not the end of their story.

The people of Judah were taken captive and marched to Babylon, where they would live in exile for fifty years. But that was not the end of their story.

And the child who would be born in a stable in Bethlehem would walk to Calvary. But that would not be the end of his story.

All of us take unwanted journeys, but God always walks with us on these journeys. God works through them and redeems them, and these difficult journeys will never be the end of our story!

In hindsight, we can see what Mary couldn't as she entered that stable, her contractions getting closer and closer together. She couldn't yet hear the angels singing, couldn't see the shepherds running to the stable, couldn't know that the magi were already on their way with their gifts to pay homage to the little king. And she certainly couldn't see that you would be reading her story two thousand years later, reflecting upon its meaning for your life.

Zechariah the prophet spoke to the people of his day who were themselves discouraged with how hard their journey had been. They were ready to give up hope. But he reminded them that one day God would send a king who would deliver his people. Then he called God's people something interesting. He called them "prisoners of hope":

> As for you also, because of the blood
>   of my covenant with you,
> I will set your prisoners free
>   from the waterless pit.
> Return to your stronghold,
>   O prisoners of hope;
> today I declare that I will restore
>   to you double. (9:11-12)

I love this line. We are all called to be prisoners of hope—captured by hope, bound by it, unable to let go of it.

Hope is a decision we make, a choice to believe that God can take the adversity, the disappointment, the heartache, and the pain of our journeys and use these to accomplish his purposes. This is precisely what we see happening in Mary's story—in the journey from Nazareth to Bethlehem and in giving birth in a stable among the animals—where we see hope born in the midst of disappointment. We want to whisper to Mary, "Don't cry. God is here, even among the animals, and people will draw hope from your story until the end of time."

I invite you, regardless of the journey you are on, to trust, to have faith, and to hope that your difficult journeys will never be the end of your story, because God is by your side. Invite God to use your disappointments to accomplish God's purposes. It was just such hope, I believe, that kept Mary going on that long, difficult journey to Bethlehem.

Reflection
The Journeys We Don't
Want to Take

In the fall of 2010, I retraced the journey of Mary and Joseph by following the most direct route from Nazareth to Bethlehem. Along the way I was struck by how difficult the journey must have been for Mary, and how disappointing.

Like Mary, all of us find ourselves forced to take journeys we do not wish to make. These journeys are not prescribed by God but by life's circumstances or the will of others. In the midst of them we may be disappointed; wonder if we've been abandoned by God; or simply feel confused as to why we've had to travel such roads. Perhaps Mary felt some of these same emotions on the journey to Bethlehem.

But here's what we find in Scripture and what is echoed in our own lives: God does not abandon us while we're on these journeys. Somehow, in ways we never anticipated, he even works through them. We look back years later and can see how God took adversity, disappointment, and pain and used these very things to accomplish his purposes.

Ann was five months pregnant when she sensed that something was not right. After an amniocentesis, doctors diagnosed her unborn baby with a genetic condition called "Chromosome 22 ring." At the time, very few other cases were known. The doctors told Ann and her husband Jerry that their child would likely be stillborn. When she asked about delivering the child early so doctors might have a chance to perform a surgery that might save his life, the doctors came back and said, "Ann, this will not be a life worth saving." Ann and Jerry would remember those words many times over the years.

Matthew was born in January 1984. Ann and Jerry chose the name *Matthew* because it means "gift from the Lord." Matthew was born with several serious birth defects, but he lived. This was not a journey Ann and

Jerry had anticipated or would have desired to make, but it was the journey life had dealt them, and they were grateful for their son.

I first met Matthew when he was eight. His mom and dad visited our church, and out of that visit our church started a ministry for Matthew and children like him, a special-needs ministry that we named after him: Matthew's Ministry. Later, when Matthew needed surgery, knowing he would need blood, his surgery prompted us to start an annual blood drive.

Matthew died at the age of twenty-one. His life shaped Ann and Jerry into two of the most remarkable people I know. And Matthew changed thousands of other lives. Today, over 140 special-needs children and adults are a part of our Matthew's Ministry. Annually in our blood drives we collect over fifteen hundred pints of blood for people in the Kansas City area. Our church and community were changed as a result of this child whose life "wasn't worth saving."

God's greatest work often arises out of the journeys we don't want to take. God has a way of wringing good from disappointment, suffering, and pain. This is what Ann and Jerry found. It is what Joseph and Mary came to see again and again. Look back over your life. Can you see how God brought good from adversity? If you are on such a journey right now, trust God to walk with you and to bring good from it.

Lord, thank you for the way you bring good from suffering. Please help me to remember that you promised never to leave me nor forsake me. Bring good from the adversity in my life, and grant me your peace when I take those journeys I don't want to take. Amen.

From *The Journey: A Season of Reflections*. Abingdon Press, 2011.

Travel Notes

The Jezreel Valley and Bethlehem

There are several routes Mary and Joseph may have taken on their journey to Bethlehem, but I believe they followed the most direct route, through the Jezreel Valley, along a road known as the Way of the Patriarchs, and on through Samaria. The route is eighty miles long.

At the beginning it goes through flat valleys that you can traverse very quickly, but the latter portions cross steep mountainsides and hills. The journey would have been planned around water sources and supplies, both for the animals and for people. Most traveled by caravan, and the trip would have taken about ten days, through the heart of what today is the Palestinian West Bank territories. Finally they would have arrived in Bethlehem.

Today in Bethlehem you can stand in Manger Square, outside the Church of the Nativity, where tradition says Jesus was born in a cave under the church. Inside, you descend to the Cave of the Nativity, where you can imagine Mary's moans, the bustle of activity, a terrified Joseph, and finally the first cries of the newborn King.

Travel Photos

Church of the Nativity, Bethlehem

Manger Square

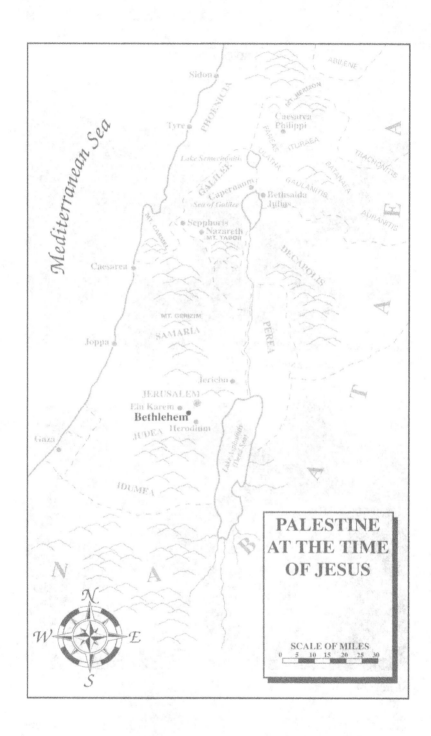

Mediterranean Sea

Sidon

Tyre

PHOENICIA

ABILENE

MT. HERMON

Caesarea
Philippi

PANEAS

ITURAEA

ULATHA

GAULANITIS

TRACHONITIS

BATANAEA

Lake Semechonitis

GALILEE

Capernaum
Sea of Galilee

Bethsaida
Julias

AURANITIS

MT. CARMEL

Sepphoris
Nazareth
MT. TABOR

DECAPOLIS

Caesarea

MT. GERIZIM

SAMARIA

PEREA

Joppa

Jericho

JERUSALEM

Ein Karem

Bethlehem

Herodium

JUDEA

Lake Asphaltitis
(Dead Sea)

Gaza

IDUMEA

N A B A T A E A

N A

**PALESTINE
AT THE TIME
OF JESUS**

W-E
S

SCALE OF MILES
0   5   10   15   20   25   30

5. The Manger

In that region there were shepherds living in the fields, keeping watch over their flock by night. Then an angel of the Lord stood before them, and the glory of the Lord shone around them, and they were terrified. But the angel said to them, "Do not be afraid; for see—I am bringing you good news of great joy for all the people: to you is born this day in the City of David a Savior, who is the Messiah, the Lord. This will be a sign for you; you will find a child wrapped in bands of cloth and lying in a manger." And suddenly there was with the angel a multitude of the heavenly host praising God and saying,

"Glory to God in the highest heaven
and on earth peace among those whom he favors!"

When the angels had left them and gone into heaven, the shepherds said to one another, "Let us go now to Bethlehem and see this thing that has taken place which the Lord has made known to us." So they went with haste and found Mary and Joseph and the child lying in a manger. When they saw this, they made known what had been told them about this child; and all who heard it were amazed at what the shepherds told them. But Mary treasured all these words and pondered them in her heart. The shepherds returned glorifying and praising God for all they had heard and seen, as it had been told them.

(Luke 2:8-20)

A Fairy Tale?

SOMETIMES WHEN WE LOOK at the Christmas story, it can seem like a fairy tale. There are lowing cattle as Mary gives birth in a barn, while the little drummer boy looks on. There are shepherds beckoned by flying angels; and soon Gaspar, Balthasar, and Melchior, riding their camels, follow the star to the barn to present their gifts of gold, frankincense, and myrrh. This version of the story makes for good Christmas carols, but did it really happen that way?

In this chapter we'll explore what may have actually happened on that first Christmas night and in the days that followed, separating what we imagine from what likely occurred. As we've done in each chapter, we'll look to see what this part of the story—the birth of Jesus and the events immediately afterward—tells us about Jesus, about God, and about ourselves.

As we look at this story in the light of history, geography, archaeology, and human experience, we begin to see that the story is anything but a fairy tale. It is gritty, difficult, and very real.

The Church of the Nativity

If you visit the Holy Land today, you will see many churches built atop holy sites and shrines. But the reality is that often we simply don't know where this or that event in the life of Jesus actually took place. These places help us remember the stories and visualize the land. Some, like the Temple Mount, the Kidron Valley, and the Mount of Olives, are easy to fix with certainty. But is there any evidence that the cave in Bethlehem beneath the Church of the Nativity is the actual birthplace of Jesus? While we cannot know for certain, the cave there does have very early attestation that it was the place of Jesus' birth.

It is believed that Emperor Hadrian had a temple to Adonis constructed on this site around A.D. 135 to discourage Christians from visiting the place. That would tell us that prior to 135, the cave was already recognized as the birthplace of Jesus. Both Justin Martyr, an early Christian leader, and the "Infancy Gospel of James," written around the middle of the second century, mention that Jesus was born in a cave in Bethlehem. By the fourth century, the Emperor Constantine, at his mother's request, built a church atop the cave to mark the birthplace of Jesus. My own sense when considering all the data is that the cave under the church may well be the actual location where Jesus was born.

The first church on this site was constructed around A.D. 326. It was later destroyed and rebuilt by Emperor Justinian in the first half of the sixth century. It is that building that still stands, though it has been remodeled on several occasions.

Outside the Church of the Nativity is Manger Square, where thousands of Christians gather every year on Christmas Eve to celebrate the birth of Jesus. To enter the church you pass through the "door of humility," low enough that you must bow to enter. At one point, it is said, the doorway was lowered to its present height to prevent nonbelievers from desecrating the church by riding their horses into it. Once inside the doorway, the long nave is surrounded by two rows of columns on either side. On the columns and the walls above them can be seen sections of frescoes from the twelfth century including, on the very top, angels between each of the windows. In the nave, to the right as one enters, is a baptismal font that dates back to the 500s, octagonal in shape as was common in early Christian baptisteries and churches.

At the front of the church is the *iconostasis*—the wall of icons that, in Eastern Orthodox churches, separates the altar from the nave where the congregation sits. Visitors line up early in the morning to pray in the place where tradition says Jesus was born. They are taken to the right side of the raised chancel, where they descend several stairs and enter the Cave of the Nativity. The cave is usually very crowded, and visitors may feel disappointed by the fact that they are hurried into and out of the cave. It is possible to move to the back of the cave and spend a bit more time, but for many the experience can feel rushed, with too little time to take it all in.

Upon descending the steps, the primary focal point is ahead and to the right. There, the visitor sees a fourteen-point star fixed to marble on the ground. Worshipers, approaching on their knees, reach in to touch the star and the circular opening in the center that connects worshipers with the stone beneath. On the star are Latin words that mean "Here Jesus Christ was born to the Virgin Mary." Was Jesus born in this very spot? We don't know, but if Jesus was born in this cave, this star provides a tangible place to pause, pray, and reflect upon the story and the mystery of the Incarnation.

Most visitors, when nudged to keep moving, rise from their knees, turn to their left a quarter-turn, then continue up another set of stairs, coming out the left side of the chancel of the church. But if, instead of moving toward the stairs, you make a 180-degree turn away from the star, you can walk to the back of the cave and linger there for a little while. There, if you close your eyes for a moment, you can imagine young Mary giving birth in this place on the first Christmas night. In your mind's eye you can picture terra cotta oil lamps on their stands, hay straw on the floor, and a midwife kneeling before Mary, who sits on a birthing stool. You can imagine Mary's cries, the bustle of activity, a terrified Joseph, and finally the first cries of the newborn King. This was no silent night. But it was most assuredly a holy night.

Before leaving the cave, as you walk back toward the star and the exit, you will notice several steps leading down into a smaller chapel to the right. This is the Chapel of the Manger. You will be reminded once more that Jesus was laid to sleep in a feeding trough used by the animals. That trough was likely not made of wood as we usually imagine it, but carved out of stone, a rectangular box where the animals ate.

As you walk up the stairs, look back at the Cave of the Nativity. Pause to marvel once more that the man hailed by one-third of the world's population as God's Son and the King of kings was born, not in a royal palace, but in the place where donkeys were kept—the equivalent of a first-century parking garage. Even today, many people would be shocked and perhaps a bit uncomfortable to hear that Jesus was born in such humble circumstances. This was no fairy tale.

The Shepherds

Let's consider the shepherds, who Luke tells us were the first to come and see this newborn King.

First-century shepherds were at the lower end of the socio-economic ladder. They were typically uneducated, usually poor, and, since they lived among their animals in the elements, sometimes smelled of dirty sheep. Because most shepherds did not own land, they grazed their flocks on the land of their neighbors. This sometimes created tension. (Imagine your neighbors regularly turning their dogs loose in your yard.) Shepherds were tolerated but not always esteemed by their neighbors. When Luke tells us that shepherds were the first to be invited to see the Christ Child, first-century hearers would not have found this endearing, but shocking!

While in Bethlehem I wanted to visit with a shepherd. My guide introduced me to a somewhat shy man named Ibrahim, who made his livelihood tending sheep. We met in an olive grove where his sheep were grazing. His wife, Fatima, and several of their children joined us. I did not see where they lived, but I saw other shepherds living in old cargo containers, and some, the Bedouins, living in tents. Others undoubtedly live in more typical homes. I also saw caves where the sheep were kept at night, with chainlink fences around the cave entrances to keep the predators out and the sheep in.

Ibrahim and Fatima had conceived seventeen times, ten of which had resulted in miscarriages or stillbirths. Four of their children and six of their sheep were with them as we sat down together under an olive tree to talk.

I was struck by Ibrahim's humility and gentleness. I was also grateful for his willingness to talk with me, a stranger, an American, and a Christian. He is a Muslim Palestinian. Muslims, as you likely know, revere Jesus and see him as a great prophet. The Quran even teaches that Jesus was born of a virgin.

I asked Ibrahim if he was familiar with the Gospel story of Jesus' birth and knew that shepherds were the first invited by God to see Jesus after his birth. He nodded his head affirmatively. Then I asked him why God invited shepherds to be the first to celebrate Jesus' birth. He quickly told me that he felt it was because shepherds were humble. He told me that Jesus was humble, and so it was fitting that God invited shepherds to his birth.

While I had always felt the same thing, hearing Ibrahim say this gave me an even clearer picture of the people who were first to see the newborn King and of the heart of God, who blessed these night-shift shepherds with such an honor.

I also found it interesting that, despite the fact (or perhaps precisely because of the fact) that shepherds were considered among the lower-ranking members of society, God referred to himself as a shepherd and to his people as his sheep. And when God chose a people for himself, God chose sheepherders. When God chose young David to be the great king over Israel, God was choosing a shepherd boy. And when God promised one day to send a new king, like David, God described that coming king as a shepherd who would search for the lost sheep. (See

Ezekiel 34.) When the child born in the stable became a man, he would describe himself as "the good shepherd" who would lay down his life for his sheep.

Once again we find the story of Jesus' birth to be not like a fairy tale or myth, but instead quite "earthy" and marked by humility.

The Angelic Chorus

I suppose one of the things that makes the story of Jesus' birth seem a bit mythological to many is the inclusion of angels. We picture winged creatures flitting about in the night sky singing, *Gloria in excelsis deo*. Or maybe we see cute babies with wings—cherubs—who are singing to the shepherds. I've never seen an angel like this, nor does it seem that this is what the shepherds likely saw that night when the angels appeared to them.

If not little cherubs singing, then what was happening that night? Let's begin by revisiting something we learned earlier: both the Hebrew and Greek words for "angel" mean "messenger." Most often in the Bible, angels simply appear as people. The writer of Hebrews encourages his readers, "Do not neglect to show hospitality to strangers, for by doing that some have entertained angels without knowing it" (Hebrews 13:2). Angels typically appear as strangers, not as winged cherubs.

In Luke's account of that first Christmas, several night-shift shepherds were watching their sheep when a stranger appeared among them. This alone might have frightened them that night, but Luke tells us there was more: "The glory of the Lord shone around them" (Luke 2:9). What did the shepherds see that night? Luke doesn't give us any more detail, and some would say that even asking this question is taking the story a bit too literally—that the mention of the "glory of the Lord" is Luke's way of telling us that God's glory was being revealed in the birth of Jesus. Whether a bright light flashed from heaven, or the moon burned particularly brightly, or the stranger reflected light, we cannot tell from the text; and it isn't Luke's point to have us focus on this. Luke wants us to notice the words of this stranger: "I am bringing you good news of great joy for all the people: to you is born this day in the city of David a Savior, who is the Messiah, the Lord" (2:10-11).

Good news of great joy for all the people—this is what the birth of Jesus is. How we crave good news of great joy! We turn on the nightly news and hear of wars, earthquakes, tornadoes, tsunamis, terrorist attacks, global warming, oil spills, and economic woes. Unlike any previous generation, we have constant access to bad news—news that produces fear and anxiety. How can we not live our lives with a constant fear buried in the recesses of our minds? The angel announced to the shepherds, "I am bringing you good news of great joy."

Today, Jesus' birth is still good news of great joy. Why? Because he is "a Savior, who is the Messiah, the Lord." To be the Messiah is to be the long-awaited King who will rule over heaven and earth. To be the Lord (a title Caesar himself claimed) was, like being the Messiah, to be sovereign, ruler, or master. But the child was not only Messiah and Lord but also Savior.

The shepherds may well have thought that this child was destined to save them from the Romans and to rule on the throne of David in Jerusalem. But Jesus was not that kind of Savior (though, had the Jews of his day listened to Jesus' teaching and chosen to love their enemies, turn the other cheek, and pray for those who persecuted them, Jerusalem would have been saved from the destruction it experienced at the hands of the Romans in A.D. 70).

If Jesus was not to lead a military charge against the Romans to save the Jews from Roman occupation, then what did he save them, and us, from?

I have asked myself this question many times. I know he is saving me (he is not finished yet!) from a life of complete narcissism. He has saved me from a life focused

We all need saving, and salvation is available for all through the child whose birth was announced that day to the shepherds.

on "more." After thirty years of marriage, I am certain he has kept me from cheating on my wife. He has saved me from becoming my worst possible self and, to whatever degree I actually seek to care for others, to give of myself for them and to work for justice and to offer compassion in a broken world. All of it is largely his doing.

Jesus saves us from guilt and shame, from hopelessness and despair, from fear and death. He "breaks the power of canceled sin, he sets the prisoner free." I have watched him save addicts from their addictions and give them a new life. I have seen him save men and women from being self-absorbed, resentful, bitter, and angry, and transform them into people who live with freedom, hope, and joy. He came to save us from the brokenness of our shared human condition and to deliver us, lead us, and send us out in his name to bring healing and hope to a broken world.

Note that this good news of great joy was for "all the people." It was not just for the Jews, but for the Gentiles too. It was good news not just for the poor shepherds, but for the wealthy wise men who were yet to come. This child would hold the key to changing the world in which we live and to saving each person who would turn to him in faith. We all need saving, and salvation is available for all through the child whose birth was announced that day to the shepherds. The glory of the Lord, whatever it may have looked like to the shepherds that night, was most clearly seen in the child who lay in the feeding trough—God in humility coming near to us, Emmanuel, to become for us "the way, and the truth, and the life" and ultimately to give his life for the human race. John, in his unique account of the Christmas story, says, "The Word became flesh and lived among us, and we have seen his glory, the glory as of a father's only son, full of grace and truth" (John 1:14).

Jesus came to save us from the bad news that seems to be all around us and to be for us "good news of great joy."

Once the stranger, the angel, announced this good news to the shepherds, suddenly there appeared out of the shadows, on the hillsides, a company of strangers. It was as though, with the announcement of this good news, the strangers could no longer keep silent and began to praise God. Like Mary when Elizabeth blessed her, these angels magnified the Lord, and their spirits rejoiced in God their Savior. Something astounding had begun in the cave in Bethlehem—yet something that would not be completed until this child walked out of another cave thirty-three years later, following his crucifixion. The company of angels shouted, "Glory to God in the highest heaven, and on earth peace among those whom he favors!" (Luke 2:14).

Glory to God and peace for humanity—this is what the shepherds saw in the birth of Jesus. This moment, when God came to the human race as a child born in poverty and obscurity to reveal God's character and will for humanity and ultimately to suffer, die, and be raised for the world, was worthy of praise and held within it the promise of peace for humankind.

When they had finished praising God, the strangers stepped back into the shadows—Luke rightly tells us they returned to heaven—and at that moment the shepherds knew they must go to Bethlehem immediately to "see this thing that has taken place, which the Lord has made known to us." When the shepherds arrived, they found everything as the messengers had told them.

And, "when they saw this, they made known what had been told them about this child; and all who heard it were amazed at what the shepherds told them" (2:15-18).

This takes us back to the angels. The angels were messengers who brought good news from God. We've learned that in the Scriptures, angels most often appear as strangers, indistinguishable from mortals. Sometimes the word *angelos* is actually used when describing mortals. Luke later tells us in 7:24 that John the Baptist sent "messengers" (*angelos*) to question Jesus. And later, in Luke 9:52, Jesus sent "messengers" before him to prepare the way for his ministry. Notice that in the story of the shepherds, after the shepherds saw Jesus they became messengers themselves, telling others what they had seen. Jesus, in the Great Commission of Matthew 28:18-20, calls his disciples (and us) to become his messengers.

I've never seen a heavenly angel, at least not that I recognized. But I have met the earthly kind of angels. I've met people who came to me at just the moment I needed them, offering a word of encouragement or help, or who otherwise blessed and sustained me, or guided and directed me. I've had the privilege of being one of these people from time to time, pointing others toward the Savior or in some way embodying the love of God or merely offering encouragement and hope.

Some years ago I asked the congregation I serve about their experience with angels. One of our choir members wrote to tell me of her experience. She had been fighting stage III ovarian cancer, and she told me how one night, thirty of her fellow choir members sneaked into her hospital room and began to sing to her. She wrote, "I believe that each of us is blessed and called to be an 'angel' throughout our lifetime. It is how we affect the lives of [others]....I had an entire chorus of angels come to me in the hospital....They lifted me with their wings of love as they sang at my bedside."

I believe in the heavenly variety of angels, but I believe they are for us a kind of example of what God expects us to be and to do. We are God's ministering agents as well, God's servants. We are called to announce the good news of Jesus Christ. We are called to offer God's peace. We are called to give glory to God. And we are called to offer hope and help, ministering to others in God's name. We are called to follow in the footsteps of angels.

One final word about the shepherds. Notice the effect Jesus had on these shepherds after they had seen him in the manger: "The shepherds returned, glorifying and praising God for all they had heard and seen" (Luke 2:20). What does that tell us about the kind of impact our encounter with Jesus might have on us today?

The Wise Men

We've been focusing on Luke's account of Jesus' birth with his emphasis on the poor and lowly. Let's return now to Matthew's account:

> In the time of King Herod, after Jesus was born in Bethlehem of Judea, wise men from the East came to Jerusalem, asking, "Where is the child who has been born king of the Jews? For we observed his star at its rising, and have come to pay him homage." When King Herod heard this, he was frightened, and all Jerusalem with him. (Matthew 2:1-3)

One thing we learn from this account is that King Herod was still alive when Jesus was born. Most scholars date Herod's death to 4 B.C., which tells us that Jesus was born no later than this (though some people have recently suggested that Herod died in 1 B.C.). For reasons we'll note in a moment, it may be that Jesus was born as much as two years before this, in 6 B.C.

How, you might ask, is it possible that Jesus was born four to six years B.C.? Doesn't B.C. mean "before Christ"? It was in the early sixth century A.D. that a monk named Dionysius Exiguus calculated the year when Jesus was born—the "year of our Lord" (*anno domini,* A.D.). It is generally recognized that Exiguus made an error in his calculations—that he was off by at least four years.

As a result of Exiguus's mistake, Jesus was actually born four to six years B.C.! It is not only our dating that is a bit off; our way of imagining what happened after Jesus' birth is typically a bit mistaken as well, particularly as it relates to the wise men. Let's consider some of the other things we learn from Matthew's story of the wise men's arrival in Bethlehem.

First, we often speak of these wise men as "kings." We sing at Christmas or Epiphany the carol "We Three Kings"—such a wonderful carol. Matthew, however, does not identify them as "kings" but as *magoi*—from which we have our English word "magician." They were probably not magicians but more likely priests who studied the stars and who believed the relative positions of the stars were signs of future events. They were something between astrologers and astronomers. These magi were likely from Persia (today's Iran) and likely followed the teachings of Zoroaster. They traveled about a thousand miles to Jerusalem to pay homage to the newborn King. Their journey would have taken three to six months.

The magi apparently saw something in the heavens that led them to conclude that a new and great king had been born in Judea. Various theories have been put forth as to what the magi actually saw. Some people have suggested that it was a comet. Others suggest that it may have been the motion of Jupiter as it seemed to align with the star Regulus and later with the planet Venus, and that perhaps at the same time its retrograde motion (its apparent movement backward in the sky, from west to east) further amplified the unique "sign" they saw in the sky. Whatever occurred, it led these magi to believe that a great king was being born in Judea.

Among the things I find fascinating about this text in Matthew is that God gave a sign to a group of truth-seekers who likely were not Jewish. God beckoned these people to Jerusalem by speaking to them in an unorthodox way—but in precisely the way that Zoroastrian priests would have been looking for! Luke's telling of the shepherd's story points toward God's concern for the humble and lowly; Matthew's telling of the magis' story points toward God's concern for all people. Jesus was not only the king and savior of the Jews but of everyone. In a sense, the magis' story parallels the story of Jonah in the Old Testament. Jonah saw the people of the ancient city of Nineveh as wicked, but God saw them as worth saving, despite the fact that they were not Jews and did not worship him.

What might the magis' story tell us about how God looks at people of other faiths? Christians are often too willing to make pronouncements about God's judgment upon those of other faiths, but this text seems to say that God deeply cares about people of other faiths. The magi ultimately foreshadow the fact that the gospel would be taken to the entire world.

Just as the angels point to God's call on our lives to be God's messengers today—demonstrating, speaking, and bringing good news of great joy to others by our words and actions—the star itself points to our role of pointing people of other faiths to Jesus. We are meant to be a compelling sign that draws others to Christ.

Let's return to the wise men. Arriving after four months of travel to the city of Jerusalem, they went to Herod's court, assuming the child must be Herod's. They asked about the child "born" king of the Jews. Herod was not a Jew, but an Idumean who had been appointed king of the Jews by Rome. But the magi were seeking a child "born king of the Jews."

Herod's response was one of fear. Who was this child that the heavens themselves declared was destined to be king? Herod's paranoia regarding his throne, and his constant fear that others were conspiring to overthrow him, is well documented. He had his favorite wife executed. He put her mother to death as well. He had his brother-in-law killed. And during the period when Jesus was born, Herod had three of his sons executed. In Matthew's account, Herod's response to the inquiry of the wise men was completely consistent with what we know of Herod during this period. Clearly Herod was a prisoner of his own paranoia and had become a tortured and confused man.

It wasn't surprising, therefore, that he responded with fear when the magi arrived with news of the child's birth. Herod sought the location of the birth, ostensibly so he could pay homage to the child. His own leaders told him that the child would have been born in Bethlehem, based upon Micah 5:2. Hearing this, Herod sent the magi to Bethlehem with instructions to return and report to him. What the magi didn't know was that Herod intended to kill the child.

When the magi finally arrived in Bethlehem after months of traveling, they found "the place where the child was," and they were "overwhelmed with joy" (Matthew 2:10b). Their response is the appropriate Christmas response, and it is one we've seen in Luke's Gospel as well surrounding the story of Jesus' birth— overwhelming joy. When we fully understand what is happening at Christmas, joy should be one of our responses.

Among my favorite moments every year at the Church of the Resurrection is Christmas Eve. We pass the candlelight throughout the room while singing "Silent Night." Following this, as the room is filled with candlelight, we pause to talk about what Christ's birth brings to us. We note that Jesus has come to bring light into our darkness, hope to our moments of despair, and salvation and deliverance to all who are burdened, bound, and oppressed. And then I say, "Once we come to understand the darkness of sin in our world, and the light that Jesus offers, we like the wise men, are overwhelmed with joy!"

At the moment the word *joy* leaves my lips, the Christmas trees are lit, the organ plays the opening notes of "Joy to the World," and the congregation breaks forth in song, singing, "Joy to the world, the Lord is come! Let earth receive her King; let every heart prepare him room, and heaven and nature sing, and heaven and nature sing, and heaven, and heaven, and nature sing." The magi, like all of us at Christmas, were "overwhelmed with joy."

Note what happens next in the story of the magi: "On entering the house, they saw the child with Mary his mother; and they knelt down and paid him homage. Then, opening their treasure chests, they offered him gifts of gold, frankincense, and myrrh" (Matthew 2:11). The magi did not enter the stable; they entered "the house." This was likely the home of Joseph's parents, which had now become Joseph and Mary's home as well.

If the magi arrived shortly after Jesus' birth, this detail lends further credence to the idea that Jesus was born in the barn attached to, under, or behind Joseph's parents' home. It is likely, however, that the magi had arrived at the home months after Jesus' birth and not the night of his birth, or even several days after. Why do we suggest this? Because Herod, in his mad attempt to kill the child whom the magi had proclaimed was born to be king of the Jews, had ordered that all the little boys two years and under be put to death "according to the time that he had learned from the wise men" (2:16c). This passage seems to indicate that from the time the magi first saw the star, two years had passed. It is possible that the star began to appear long before the birth of Jesus; but if it began to appear with the birth of Jesus, then Jesus may have been nearly two years old when the magi visited him, hence the possibility that Jesus was born as early as 6 B.C.

Matthew includes the story of the "slaughter of the innocents" in 2:16-17. We often imagine that hundreds of children were put to death, but in a town the size of Bethlehem it may be that only a dozen or so children were killed by Herod's men. By this time Joseph had been warned by God in a dream to take Mary and Jesus to Egypt to escape Herod's wrath. Joseph, Mary, and Jesus become refugees and aliens in Egypt during this time. When I think of this story, I can't help but think of the many immigrants, both legal and illegal, who flee to the United States either in fear for their lives in their home country, or in hopes of a better future. Jesus was a child taken into Egypt as an alien, a refugee.

One last word about the magi: While Luke helps us see the lowliness of Jesus' birth and emphasizes God's concern for the humble shepherds, Matthew helps us see that the rich, too, are invited by God to pay homage to Jesus. The affluent magi brought gifts to honor Jesus—gold, frankincense, and myrrh. These gifts have been seen as symbolic of the three roles that Jesus was born to play: gold was the gift of kings, frankincense was offered by the priests with certain sacrifices, and myrrh was used in preparing the dead for burial. Jesus was born to be both king and priest, and he would one day give his life for the sins of the world (after which his body would be anointed with myrrh before burial).

On Christmas Eve, as I mentioned earlier, we invite our congregation to follow the example of the wise men by giving of what is precious to them as an expression of their joy and gratitude for the birth of Jesus and his role in their lives. For some who are struggling financially, the gift may be something small, but all are invited to give something as they are able. These gifts are then used for projects benefiting children in poverty, divided equally between projects in the developing world (currently Africa) and in our own inner city. This Christmas Eve offering has become one of our most meaningful traditions. Even those who are not religious find this to be a moving part of the service.

Mike Slaughter, pastor of the Ginghamsburg United Methodist Church, reminds his congregation each year that "Christmas is not your birthday!" Consider giving a special offering this Christmas for people in need. If you have children, teach them this tradition, and help them learn that Christmas is not primarily about what is under the tree but about God's gift of Jesus Christ, and, in turn, Christ's call upon our lives to give ourselves for others.

Was Jesus Born on December 25?

Before concluding our study of Christmas, I'd like to answer a question and to consider the Christmas story as told by the Gospel of John.

The question is simply this: "Was Jesus born on December 25?" The answer is that no one knows when Jesus was born. Jewish people did not mark birthdays in the same way we do today. Some even considered it sacrilege. Recalling the exact date that Jesus was born is not nearly as important as recalling the date of his death. (Matthew, Mark, and Luke note that he was crucified on the day of Passover, and John tells us that Jesus was crucified on the day of preparation for the Passover when the Passover lambs were sacrificed.) If we don't know when Jesus was born, why do we celebrate his birth on December 25?

Occasionally you may meet Christians who refuse to celebrate Christmas, telling you that Christmas was first a pagan holiday. In a sense they are right. In the old Julian calendar, December 24/25 was the date for the winter solstice, the longest night of the year. After this night, the days would begin to grow longer and the nights shorter. Ancient people celebrated this date; it meant the end of gloom and darkness and the victory of the sun and the light over that darkness.

Many believe that when Christians in the fourth century settled on a date to celebrate the birth of Jesus, they chose the date not because it was a pagan holiday, but because the heavens themselves declared at this time the truth of the gospel. The winter solstice represented astronomically what John's Gospel proclaimed was happening spiritually in the birth of Jesus Christ. Just as darkness was defeated by light, so in Jesus, God's light would defeat the darkness of sin and death.

This meaning is captured in John's telling of the story. John doesn't mention angels or shepherds or wise men; he speaks only of light and life and the defeat of darkness. John writes, "In the beginning was the Word, and the Word was with God, and the Word was God. He was in the beginning with God. All things came into being through him, and without him not one thing came into being. What has come into being in him was life, and the life was the light of all people. The light shines in the darkness, and the darkness did not overcome it" (John 1:1-5).

Every year at our Christmas Eve service, we read John 1:1-18 as we darken the sanctuary and watch as the Christ light (a large candle) is brought in. Then we pass the flame throughout the sanctuary from the Christ light to smaller candles held by everyone. We turn to the person next to us and say, as we light their candle, "The light of Christ." What better date to celebrate the birth of Jesus, the light of the world, than on the night the heavens themselves dramatize the defeat of darkness by light? (If you don't have candlelight Christmas Eve services, please join our church online that night at www.cor.org. Have a candle and matches ready so you can join us in the candlelighting!)

The Manger: Where God's Creatures Come to Eat

Let's return to Luke's account of the Christmas story and his mention of the manger. While in the Holy Land, in the town of Bethlehem, I saw something as I read Luke's account of that first Christmas that I had never seen in thirty years of reading the story. I don't know how I had missed it before. It was the idea that Jesus slept that first night in a feeding trough. I knew this detail but had seen in it only the humility the feeding trough represented. But this year I noticed that Luke mentions the manger three times. In Luke 2:7, we're told that the child was laid in a manger. Then in Luke 2:12, the angel announced to the shepherds that the Christ was born and "this will be a sign to you: you will find a child wrapped in bands of cloths and lying in a manger." And in Luke 2:16, the shepherds found the child "lying in the manger." I began to see that perhaps the manger was not only a sign to the shepherds, but for us also.

The manger or feeding trough is not just a sign of Jesus' humility. A feeding trough is where God's creatures come to eat. This is a sign to us—it is a detail Luke includes to point toward something greater. Moses said, "One does not live by bread alone" (Deuteronomy 8:3). Moses meant that there was something deeper we hunger for. Isaiah the prophet once asked, "Why do you spend your money for that which is not bread, / and your labor for that which does not satisfy?" (Isaiah 55:2). Isaiah was pointing, with Moses, to a deeper hunger we have as human beings, but also to our tendency to spend money and to work hard for that which cannot ultimately satisfy our hunger. Jesus, I believe, alluded to these two verses when he said, "I am the bread of life. Whoever comes to me will never be hungry, and whoever believes in me will never be thirsty" (John 6:35). At the Last Supper, Jesus took bread and said, "This is my body, which is given for you" (Luke 22:19b).

He who called himself the bread of life, who alone can satisfy the deepest longings of our souls, was born in the town of Bethlehem—the "House of Bread"—and was laid to sleep on that first night in a trough where God's creatures ate.

What we really hunger for will not be found under the tree on Christmas morning. We hunger for meaning, for joy, for hope in the face of despair. We hunger to know that we can be forgiven and start anew after things we regret. We hunger for a love that will not let us go and for life and triumph in the face of death. These come through a baby born in a stable, laid to sleep in a feeding trough, visited by night-shift shepherds. He is for us the bread of life. And we must come to the stable to satisfy the deepest desires of our hearts.

I invite you to come to the manger this Christmas and to eat of this bread. I invite you to choose to become Christ's follower and to put your trust in him. John tells us that "all who received him, who believed in his name, he gave power to become children of God" (1:12).

Christmas is the perfect time to call out to God and to his son Jesus Christ and to pray, "Jesus, I come to you, like the shepherds and the magi did so long ago. I accept you as my King, my Savior, and my Lord. Forgive me for the ways I've turned from God's path, and help me to follow you. Save me from myself, and help me to live for you. I receive you, Jesus Christ, and believe in your name. Make me your child, and bring me your joy. Help me to do justice, to love kindness, and to walk humbly with you. In your name I pray, Jesus my Christ. Amen."

Reflection
The Shepherds' Response

The shepherds had heard from heavenly messengers that a new king had been born in Bethlehem. They would find him in a parking garage (that's what a stable was), lying in a bed of straw where the animals ate.

How would the shepherds respond? Would they stay in their fields; or would they leave their flocks, risk losing their jobs, and hike over the hillsides to Bethlehem in search of the newborn King? Scripture tells us what they did: The shepherds "went with haste" to see the one whose birth would be a source of "good news of great joy for all the people."

When the shepherds arrived, they saw with their own eyes "Mary and Joseph and the child lying in the manger," and they became God's messengers—God's angels—telling others about the child. This is important. It demonstrates a rhythm in the Christian life: Others tell us about Jesus, we see with our own eyes and believe, and we tell others what we've seen. Then we return to our daily lives with joy, changed forever.

It is Christmas time, and there are many people who typically don't go to church but are searching nonetheless for the "good news of great joy for all the people." They've been searching at the mall, at their Christmas parties, even sitting in front of a decorated Christmas tree, but they still haven't found Christmas. And they won't find it, unless someone plays the part of the angel and invites them to come and see the child wrapped in swaddling clothes and lying in a manger.

Ann's husband invited her to attend our candlelight Christmas Eve services one year. She wrote, "If my husband hadn't invited me to Church of the Resurrection, I would still be searching for a way to fill the hole in my heart that God now fills." That was many years ago; today, Ann has gone on to become a leader in our congregation.

Each year, we give away our entire Christmas Eve offering to two projects benefiting children in poverty.

Half of the funds last year went to projects in Malawi, Africa, and the other half to renovate and support inner-city schools. Ann has become one of the leaders in our work with the inner-city schools, which includes tutoring, installing playgrounds, repainting buildings, and supporting teachers.

After we had completed a playground at one of the inner-city schools, a man at the school asked Ann, "Why would you do this for us?" She told him, "It's our way of showing God's love for you." Both began to cry as they stood on the playground that day.

Ann's angel was her husband, who invited her to "come and see." She came on Christmas Eve and heard the story of the child, born in a barn, who slept in a feeding trough. She discovered the "good news of great joy that was for all the people." When Ann returned home, "singing and praising God," she went on to became a messenger who has shared God's love with hundreds of others. The world was changed because of that one invitation.

Christmas is God's gift to us—a gift of light and life, hope and grace. The gift is a reflection of God's concern for the world, and God's desire to heal it and drive away its darkness. The gift of Christmas, therefore, comes with a mission, a calling, and a responsibility. We must bear Christ's light into the world by our love expressed through works of mercy and justice. At Christmas we are invited to receive Christ's light, but not only to receive it. We are invited to bear the light, to walk in the light, and to take the light into the world.

Lord, I accept your light, your love, your mercy, and your grace. Help me to hear the "good news of great joy" that you have come to us in Jesus Christ. Then make me one of your messengers, taking your light into the world. Amen.

———————————————

From *The Journey: A Season of Reflections.* Abingdon Press, 2011.

Travel Notes

A Modern-Day Shepherd

Luke tells us it was shepherds who were first invited to see the newborn king. Today we can go to the shepherds' fields, overlooking Bethlehem, to see a place very much like the one where the angels heard God's "good news of great joy," and we can meet shepherds who may not be very different from those shepherds.

In my travels to the Holy Land, I met a shepherd named Ibrahim, and this is what he told me:

> I've loved doing this since I was a little boy. Someone who is humble can talk to others who are humble like them. Perhaps he was announced to shepherds to demonstrate that humility to others. Look where he was born—in a manger, where sheep eat. So that's why there's a connection between someone who is humble and Jesus Christ. In the moment he was born, he was humble.

When I think of the story of the shepherds who were the first to celebrate the birth of Jesus, I can't help but think of Ibrahim.

Travel Photos

Bethlehem

Shepherd

Notes

Chapter 1
1. "Who Wants to Be Mary?" by Christian Coon, *The Christian Century*, Dec. 15, 2008. http://www.christiancentury.org/blogs/archive/2008-12/who-wants-be-mary. Accessed April 19, 2011.

Chapter 3
1. William Barclay, *The Gospel of Luke: The New Daily Study Bible* (Westminster John Knox, 2001), p. 17.
2. If you are interested in setting up this type of Christmas offering at your church, visit the Web site set up for this book: www.JourneyThisChristmas.com. The site has a variety of resources related to the book, including information about how churches and other groups can celebrate Christmas.

Chapter 4
1. One study Bible makes the statement that Mary and Joseph's journey from Nazareth to Bethlehem would have been at least a "three-day trip." But three days would have been impossible. As the crow flies, the journey was seventy miles; but traveling between Nazareth and Bethlehem was not "as the crow flies." The Way of the Patriarchs traversed mountain ridges with switchbacks and journeyed east and then west. One might be able to travel fifteen miles in a day on foot and by donkey through the flat Jezreel Valley, but over the mountains one might make only eight miles in a day. Keep in mind that a day ended at the last water spot one could reach before nightfall. My own calculations, based upon the short sections I walked and the terrain we traversed, show that Mary and Joseph's trip probably took eight to ten days. A BBC journalist walked this same path several years ago and took ten days. A Palestinian company will take you on this journey, and they allow ten days as well.

Acknowledgments

Special thanks to Alex Schwindt, the videographer and editor who traveled with me in the Holy Land. Through his work, many people will have a chance to see and experience the Holy Land and glean fresh insights into the Christmas story. Thank you, Alex.

I also want to thank James Ridgeway at Educational Opportunities, Inc. EO has been leading tours of the Holy Land since 1973, and this project would not have been possible without their generous support and connections in Israel.

Finally, thanks to the people of The United Methodist Church of the Resurrection, whom I am privileged to pastor. This book began as a sermon series, and the reflections that accompany it were inspired by my work with them.

About the Author

ADAM HAMILTON is senior pastor of The United Methodist Church of the Resurrection in the Kansas City area with an average weekly attendance of over 10,000. It has been cited as the most influential mainline church in America. Hamilton speaks across the U.S. each year on leadership and connecting with nonreligious and nominally religious people. In 2013 the White House invited him to preach at the National Prayer Service as part of the presidential inauguration festivities. In 2016 he was appointed to the President's Advisory Council on Faith-Based and Neighborhood Partnerships.

A master at explaining questions of faith in a down-to-earth fashion, he is the author of many books including *The Journey, The Way, 24 Hours That Changed the World, Enough, Why: Making Sense of God's Will, When Christians Get it Wrong, Seeing Gray in a World of Black and White, Forgiveness, Love to Stay, Making Sense of the Bible,* and *Half Truths.* To learn more about Adam and to follow his regular blog postings, visit www.AdamHamilton.org.

THE JOURNEY

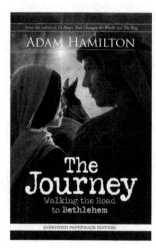

Journey with Adam Hamilton as he travels from Nazareth to Bethlehem in this fascinating look at the birth of Jesus Christ. As he did with Jesus' crucifixion in *24 Hours That Changed the World*, Hamilton once again approaches a world-changing event with thoughtfulness. Using historical information, archaeological data, and a personal look at some of the stories surrounding the birth, the most amazing moment in history will become more real and heartfelt as you walk along this road.

Read *The Journey* on your own or, for a more in-depth study, enjoy it with a small group.

ISBN 978-1-5018-2879-9

CONTINUE THE JOURNEY

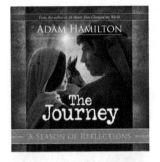

Go deeper on your Christmas journey with *A Season of Reflection*. With Scripture, stories, and prayer, this collection of 28 daily readings brings the well-known story into your daily spiritual life.

ISBN 978-1-4267-1426-9

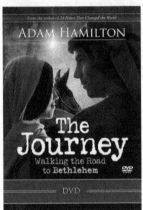

Join Adam Hamilton as he travels the roads to Bethlehem in this video journey. In five video segments, Adam explores Bethlehem, the routes the Holy Family traveled, the traditional site of the stable in Bethlehem, the ruins of Herodium, and more.

ISBN 978-1-4267-1999-8

A small group leader guide, study resources for children and youth, and an app for families are also available.
Learn more at JourneyThisChristmas.com

ŀ Abingdon Press™

Available wherever fine books are sold.
For more information about Adam Hamilton, visit www.AdamHamilton.org.

THE WAY

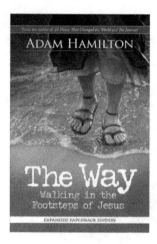

Travel to the Holy Land in this third volume of Adam Hamilton's Bible study trilogy on the life of Jesus. Once again, Hamilton approaches his subject matter with thoughtfulness and wisdom as he did with Jesus' crucifixion in *24 Hours That Changed the World* and with Jesus' birth in *The Journey*. Using historical background, archaeological findings, and stories of the faith, Hamilton retraces the footsteps of Jesus from his baptism to the temptations to the heart of his ministry, including the people he loved, the enemies he made, the parables he taught, and the roads that he traveled.

Read *The Way* on your own or, for a more in-depth study, enjoy it with a small group.

ISBN 978-1-5018-2878-2

Available wherever fine books are sold.
For more information about Adam Hamilton, visit www.AdamHamilton.org.

CONTINUE THE WAY

This companion volume to *The Way* functions beautifully on its own or as part of the churchwide experience. Adam Hamilton offers daily devotions that enable us to pause, meditate, and emerge changed forever. Ideal for use during Lent, the reflections include Scripture, stories from Hamilton's own ministry, and prayers.

ISBN 978-1-4267-5252-0

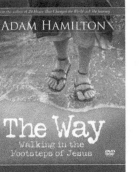

Join Adam Hamilton in the Holy Land as he retraces the life and ministry of Jesus Christ in this DVD study. Perfect for adult and youth classes, each session averages ten minutes.

ISBN 978-1-4267-5253-7

A small group leader guide and
study resources for children and youth are also available.

Available wherever fine books are sold.
For more information about Adam Hamilton, visit www.AdamHamilton.org.

24 HOURS THAT CHANGED THE WORLD

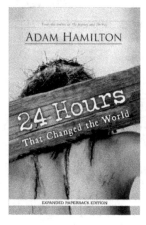

Walk with Jesus on his final day.
Sit beside him at the Last Supper.
Pray with him in Gethsemane.
Follow him to the cross.
Desert him. Deny him.
Experience the Resurrection.

No single event in human history has received more attention than the suffering and crucifixion of Jesus of Nazareth. In this heartbreaking, inspiring book, Adam Hamilton guides us, step by step, through the last 24 hours of Jesus' life.

ISBN 978-1-5018-2877-5

"Adam Hamilton combines biblical story, historical detail, theological analysis, and spiritual insight, and pastoral warmth to retell the narrative of Jesus' last and greatest hours."

—**Leith Anderson,** author of *The Jesus Revolution*

Available wherever fine books are sold.
For more information about Adam Hamilton, visit www.AdamHamilton.org.

CONTINUE 24 HOURS

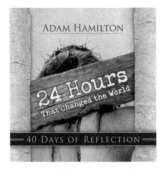

These devotions are ideal for use during Lent or any other time of the year. With Scripture, reflection on the events of Jesus' final day, stories from Hamilton's own ministry, and prayer, these devotions can be used alone or as a companion to the book.

ISBN 978-1-4267-0031-6

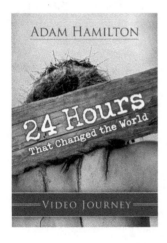

Travel with Adam Hamilton through this companion DVD visiting the sites, walking where Jesus walked along the road that led to the pain and triumph of the cross.

The DVD includes seven sessions plus an introduction and bonus clips. Each session averages ten minutes.

ISBN 978-0-687-65970-8

Also available:
A leader guide for small groups,
older and younger children's study sessions,
and youth small group resources

Abingdon Press™

Available wherever fine books are sold.
For more information about Adam Hamilton, visit www.AdamHamilton.org.

CPSIA information can be obtained
at www.ICGtesting.com
Printed in the USA
LVHW012226131119
637285LV00007B/7